Sell Like Titans

How to Transform Your Business by Understanding Consumer Behavior; and Psychology of Persuasion, Marketing, Motivation, Choice, Advertising, and Branding Like World Class Marketers

Sam Amoo

The information contained herein is provided solely for informational purposes and is therefore universal. The information is presented without contract or assurance of any kind.
The trademarks are used without the trademark owner's consent, and the trademark is published without the trademark owner's permission or support. All trademarks and brands mentioned in this book are solely for clarity purposes and are owned by their respective owners, who are not affiliated with this document.
For Questions and enquiries contact; sam@samamoo.com
ISBN: 978-1-63750-353-9

Sam Amoo Publishing

Special Bonus

SPECIAL BONUS!

Want These 2 Bonus EBooks For Free?

Get FREE, Unlimited Access To These and All of Our New Books By Joining Our Community

SCAN

Scan With Your Camera to Join

Other Books

- How to be More in Tune with The Feelings of Your Customers
- Time Management For Busy People

Table of Contents

SELL LIKE TITANS **1**

S P E C I A L   B O N U S **4**

O T H E R   B O O K S **5**

INTRODUCTION **8**

CHAPTER 1 .... **15**

UNDERSTANDING YOUR CUSTOMERS 15

The Anatomy of Consumer Decision Making *15*

The Four Stages of the Purchase Cycle *20*

CHAPTER 2 .... **40**

HOW TO MANAGE CONSUMER EXPECTATIONS 40

CHAPTER 3 .... **44**

CREATING A STRONG BRAND 44

How Important is a Strong Brand to Your Business? *47*

Why a Brand is Important to Your Business *52*

The Three Components of a Brand. *56*

The Benefits of Building a Strong Brand. *61*

How to Tell a Brand Story that Resonates *62*

CHAPTER 4 .... **67**

PROBLEM SOLVING TECHNIQUES THAT WORKS 67

Identify the Problem *67*

Analyze the Problem *71*

Describe the Problem *74*

Look for Root Causes *76*

Develop Alternate Solutions *84*

Implement the Solution *87*

Measure the Results *91*

Repetition and Consistency *92*

CHAPTER 5 .... **95**

THE PSYCHOLOGY OF MARKETING 95

UNDERSTANDING HUMAN BEHAVIOR 99

Cognitive Psychology ... *101*
Cognitive Psychology of Marketing ... *103*
How Cognitive Psychology can Help us Sell more products? ... *106*
Why is Cognitive Psychology Used in Marketing? ... *111*
UNDERSTANDING YOUR CUSTOMERS ... 114
12 Psychological Bases that Drive Customer Behavior ... *114*

CHAPTER 6 ... **116**

THE PSYCHOLOGY OF MOTIVATION ... 116

CHAPTER 7 ... **121**

THE PSYCHOLOGY OF PERSUASION ... 121

CHAPTER 8 ... **130**

THE PSYCHOLOGY OF CHOICE ... 130
What is Psychology of Choice? ... *131*
What You Should Know About Choices ... *132*

CHAPTER 9 ... **138**

THE PSYCHOLOGY OF ADVERTISING ... 138

CHAPTER 10 ... **150**

THE PSYCHOLOGY OF BRANDING ... 150
Brand Management ... *151*
Why does a Brand Matter? ... *152*
How to Create a Good Brand ... *155*
How can You Build a Brand? ... *156*

SPECIAL BONUS ... **159**

THANK YOU! ... **160**

ABOUT THE AUTHOR ... **162**

OTHER BOOKS ... **163**

Introduction

Every business owner knows that the key to succeeding in today's economy is to build a brand that resonates with consumers. But many business owners struggle with how to make their brand speak to their target audience, how to gain attention, and how to turn prospects into buyers.

This book reveals the everyday marketing tactics, routines and habits of billionaires, and world-class performers and marketers - *how they get their message across, who they're trying to attract, and why.* Using the insights shared by these people, you'll discover how to build a successful brand that resonates with your audience, attracts attention, and ultimately convert prospects into buyers.

How do you sell like crazy?

H*ow can you create an irresistible offer that will leave your buyers wanting more?*

The most successful people are those who know how to inspire and motivate others to do what they need them to do. If you want to make your sales skyrocket, you must understand why people buy, not just what they'll buy.

Are you one of many people struggling to grow their

business?

Most likely you are not in the top 5% of your local market. You probably have a limited budget and don't have the resources to do what is necessary to grow your business. And you probably struggle to compete with the giants in your industry.

Selling like a Titan isn't easy. It's time to stop feeling like a beginner. You are not alone. You have much to learn about marketing, sales, and customer service, but that doesn't mean that you should be ignored or overlooked.

In this book, you will be given the strategies, routines, and habits of people like *Mark Cuban, Oprah Winfrey, Dr. Phil McGraw, and Tony Robbins.* Their successes have been built on their everyday marketing tactics, routines, and habits.

This book will show you how to transform your business and become a champion in your industry by building on their successes and learning from their marketing tactics.

The book includes step-by-step instructions that will show you how to turn your marketing efforts into sales.

Sell Like Titans teach you how to put yourself on the path to becoming the greatest businessperson you can possibly be. By doing so, you will not only become a business icon, but you will learn how to master the skills and disciplines required to attract clients and customers at the highest level.

The psychology of marketing is a vital part of any business, but often, it's something that is overlooked or even ignored completely. It can be very difficult for a business owner to understand why their customers aren't responding to their marketing efforts, and then make changes to improve their business. The psychology of marketing helps us understand our customers and how we can best reach them.

What happens when you combine the powerful, yet the counterintuitive concept of *"love bombing"* with marketing psychology? You get *"Amazing result and sales."*

If you were to ask a typical entrepreneur what their biggest challenge is when it comes to selling, the number one answer would most likely be: *getting people to buy.*

It doesn't matter if your product solves a major problem for customers, or whether you've spent months building an entirely new product or service. No matter how hard you work, it's not enough to just get the word out about your products. You also have to make sure that your customers are able to buy your product and be converted to return customers. In other words, you need to get them to take action.

The problem with this challenge is that it's so simple in nature that it's easy to feel like you don't have to do anything special to get people to buy. But, as many entrepreneurs know, you can't afford to rest on your laurels when it comes to selling. If you want to scale and build a long-term business, then you need to do more than just get the word out. You need to get into the head of your potential clients and customers to get them to buy repeatedly from you.

In a world where millions of small businesses struggle to make money and reach their potential, one of the biggest problems they face is selling themselves and their services. We're talking about building and selling relationships, not products. You can either be part of the problem or the solution.

The truth is that you have to be more than just a business to make sales.

You need to be a human being with the ability to listen, empathize, motivate, persuade and negotiate.

Most of us have heard the saying that *"people buy from people."* But most of us don't know how to build and sell relationships.

When it comes to marketing, there are so many different strategies available to you. However, it can be difficult to know which is the best way to go about marketing your business. This book will teach you about the psychology of marketing so that you can make informed decisions about your marketing strategy.

There's a difference between a good product and a great product. While it's a little cliché to say, "it's all about the buyer experience" (a concept that seems to be losing its relevance as of late), there is something to be said for creating a positive customer experience. In fact, if you've ever spent time trying to sell a product to someone—you'll know that most people have no interest in buying anything they don't want or need. When you create an experience where your potential customers feel comfortable and satisfied, they're more likely to buy your products—no matter what they are.

The key to making this happen is to take the time to understand your buyers' needs. For some companies, this might be fairly easy; they sell products that are straightforward and simple to use. But for others, it can be quite challenging. In order to sell products that meet their customers' needs, you have to get inside their heads and see things from their perspective.

We're going to look at the psychology of why people buy things and how to use that knowledge to sell like crazy.

The psychology of marketing is all about understanding the psychology of your audience and how you can use this knowledge to get the best results out of them. It is also about understanding our customers and how we can best reach them. If you think about it, there's a reason why some products succeed and others fail.

Success is often not a matter of luck it's a matter of applying the right psychology to persuade your audience to make a purchase. It's a simple concept, but not always easy to execute.

"I've been an entrepreneur for over a decade now. In that time, I learned a lot about business and marketing.

In this book, I share the knowledge I've gained through years of study and experience, and explain how to use it to make your business a success. If you want to grow your business—and if you want to make it into the big leagues—you need to learn how to market to the right audience, at the right time, with the right message.

This book offers marketers, entrepreneurs, and business owners the ability to develop a marketing system to reach the next level.

I believe we have the opportunity to shape the future of marketing by applying the everyday tactics, routines, and habits of billionaires, icons, and world-class performers. To do this we need to change how we think about our marketing strategies and approach.

In this book, we'll learn what the billionaires, icons, and world-class marketers do every day to turn their marketing into everyday sales machine.

Chapter 1

Understanding Your Customers

The Anatomy of Consumer Decision Making

A new study from the University of Pennsylvania has found that people have a *"rule of thumb"* when it comes to their decisions. The study shows that consumers tend to make decisions based on simple, quick rules of thumb, rather than complex analysis of the situation at hand.

This is very interesting to me because I've often wondered why people don't seem to use analytical techniques when making important purchases. Without a doubt, the decision to buy something is a complex one, and it's not always easy to make the right choice.

However, the research shows that when people are faced with a decision, they tend to make decisions based on simple, quick rules of thumb.

Why is this?

The researchers say that it's because people want to be able to make decisions quickly and easily. So, when they're faced with a decision, they make a snap judgment based on their rule of thumb. And, this is a good thing. It's what keeps us safe. It's what makes us avoid getting into a car accident. And it's what allows us to survive.

But, the problem with this is that we often make decisions based on our gut feelings rather than our head. This means that we're not making the best decisions for ourselves.

So, what can we do to make better decisions? How can we make sure that we're making the right decisions for ourselves?

The answer is that we need to use our analytical skills to make the best decisions for ourselves. When we make a decision, we have to consider all of the pros and cons of that decision. The thing is that the pros and cons of a decision are often hidden and unseen.

Since they're often not obvious, we tend to make a decision based on our gut feelings. This is a problem because, as we'll see later in the book, the decisions we make based on our gut feelings often aren't the best ones.

The first step to using your *analytical skills* is to understand what you're looking for in a decision. For example, if you're buying a new car, you need to consider the following:

- What do you want to use the car for?
- What are the things that are important to you?

- What do you want to do with the car?
- What kind of car can you afford?
- How do you want to feel when you're driving the car?
- How safe do you want the car to be?
- Where do you want to drive it?
- How much time will you spend driving it?
- Will the car work for you?
- What is the best car for your needs?
- What are the things that you don't want in the car?
- Are there any other important factors to consider?

The more detailed the answer, the better the decision.

Now, once you have a list of factors to consider, the next step is to figure out what is most important. In other words, which of the factors are most important to you?

For example, if you have the following choices:

A: You get a great deal on a new car, but it doesn't have cruise control.

B: You get a great deal on a new car, but it doesn't have power steering.

C: You get a good deal on a new car with no power steering and cruise control.

D: You get a new car, and it has power steering and cruise control.

Which one is the best choice for you? The answer is **D**. Option D is the best choice because power steering and cruise control are more important than the price of the car. If you don't know what to do next, here are some tips to help you make a decision:
Try to simplify the decision by eliminating any factors that aren't important to you. If you can't eliminate any factors, then try to come up with a list of things that are most important to you. If you still can't narrow the list down to one or two choices, then ask yourself what is most important. This is called **making a trade-off**.

For example, if you have three choices (**A**, **B**, and **C**) and **A** is a great deal on a car that doesn't have cruise control, but **B** is a great deal on a car that doesn't have power steering and **C** is a great deal on a car with no power steering and cruise control, which one is more important to you?
If you want to make sure that you make the right choice, then make sure that you look at the entire list of factors

before you make a final decision. In other words, don't just consider the price and make a choice based on that. Also, remember that price is only one factor and there are other factors that you need to consider.

There are two types of decision-making: **analytical and intuitive**.

Analytical decision-making *involves using facts and figures to make a decision.* For example, you can calculate the price difference between **A** and **B**.

You can compare the price of **B** to **C**. You can calculate how much money you will save by buying from **A** rather than from **B**.

Analytical thinking is a key part of being successful in life. But *if you want to become a good decision-maker, you need to become better at analytical thinking.*

Intuitive decision-making *involves relying on feelings or instincts instead of facts and figures.* For example, if you're trying to decide between **A** and **B**, then you might want to try to decide by feeling how much you like each of the choices. This is called *heuristics*. ***Heuristics*** is one of the reasons why people are so good at making decisions. However, heuristics also means that your decisions may not be the best possible choice.

The Four Stages of the Purchase Cycle

Whether you are an established company or a new entrant, your decision to enter the market will be influenced by many factors. It is important that you plan well before embarking on the purchase process. The first step in any business venture is to define your market niche and identify your product/service offerings. Your market niche should be well defined, and if it is not, you will be unable to achieve the market share required to succeed.

Once you have established your niche, you need to ensure that you have a product/service that is differentiated from your competitors. This will help you to stand out in the marketplace and gain market share.

The next step is to develop your marketing strategy. You need to ensure that you develop a marketing strategy that will help you to sell your product/service to your target market. Developing a marketing strategy will help you to understand the needs of your target market and create a marketing mix that will best meet those needs.

The marketing mix includes the following elements:

Market research: This involves conducting qualitative and quantitative studies to identify your target market, as well as their demographic and psychographic characteristics. This information will be used to design the marketing mix and help you to understand your customer's needs.

Product development: This involves developing new products and services to meet the needs of your customers. Your product or service may include a new product or an improvement on an existing product. It may also be a completely new product that is aimed at a new market. Your product development process will involve *research, design, and development.*

Other elements of the marketing mix are; The right price, the right product or service, the right place, the right time, the right message, the right communication channels, and the right customer.

This is a time-consuming exercise and I have put together resourceful information below to help you through the four major stages of the purchase cycle.

Stage 1: Researching Your Market

The first stage of the purchase cycle is all about research. If you are considering acquiring a business, it is vital that you understand the business you are looking at. You need to understand the challenges they face and the opportunities they can create for you. You also need to determine whether the acquisition is right for you. There are a number of ways to conduct market research. You can use the services of a specialist commercial research company or, if you are not sure about their methodology, you could undertake your own in-house research.

Researching the Market **-** The research process begins with a thorough understanding of your target market. You must know what makes this market tick.

How do they live? What are their needs? Where are they? Who are your competitors?

Once you have an understanding of your target market, you need to develop a good grasp of what you want to sell them. It is important to note that your product should be in line with the needs of your market.

What are the benefits to your customers? How does it solve their problems? Is it easy for them to use? Is it affordable?

If you can answer all these questions, you are ready to begin the research process.

Research Methods - As mentioned earlier, the research process begins with a thorough understanding of your target market. Once you have an idea of what you want to sell them, you will need to conduct primary research to discover more about your market.

What is the competition like?

How do they compare to you?

Are they similar to your target market?

Do they have the same needs?

You need to find out as much as you can about the market and its players in order to make an informed decision about how to enter it.

This stage includes:

- Identifying and understanding your main competitors.
- Identify the needs and problems of your prospective

customers.

- Finding out more about the local political, economic and regulatory environment.
- Identifying the best entry points into the market.

In other words, before you start making a pitch to clients or investors, you need to know all about them.

Stage 2: Defining Your Strategy

The second stage involves defining a strategy for entering the market. This is where you decide which channels to use and what you are going to do to enter the market.

After all, if you are going to sell your product or service, the next step is to determine how to sell it. There are different ways to do this. You can advertise your product or service in the local newspapers and magazines. You can also place an advertisement on the internet via the social media platforms like **Facebook, YouTube, Instagram, Reddit, Twitter, Quora, TikTok, etc.**

If you plan to sell a physical product, then you will have to determine the price of your product and how you are going to deliver it.

Once you have determined that you want to launch your own business, it's time to determine when you are going to launch.

This is when you should be able to answer these questions:

What am I doing?

What is the product or service I am offering?

How am I going to market my business?

What is my strategy for selling the product or service?

How am I going to deliver the product or service?

How am I going to price the product or service?

How am I going to manage the customer relationships?

If you are still not sure when you are ready, here are some questions you can ask yourself to help you make this decision.

- Am I financially prepared?
- Do I have a good idea about how to make money?
- Am I prepared to take the risk and invest in my business?
- Am I willing to make mistakes?
- Am I ready to put in long hours?
- Am I ready to make sacrifices?
- Am I ready to work hard for the first few years of

my business?

- Am I ready to learn everything I need to know about my business?

If you answered **YES** to all of these questions, then you are ready to launch your own business. But if you answered **NO** to any of them, then you may want to rethink your decision and reconsider going through with starting a business.

In fact, a great way to determine if your business is ready to be launched is to start thinking about your future plans for your business. Once you have determined what you plan to do after you launch your business, you will have a better idea of whether or not you are ready. If you answered yes to all of the above questions, then it's time to get started on your business. You can either create a physical product or service and sell it, or you can sell a digital product or service and make money from the sale.

Regardless of which option you choose, you will need to decide on your pricing model. Your pricing model will dictate how you are going to set your prices for your product or service. There are three types of pricing models:

Fixed pricing: This is when the price of the product or service is determined before you launch. Fixed pricing means that you determine your price before you launch and you don't change it unless you make a significant change to your business.

Variable pricing: This is when you determine your price after you launch. The price you set after you launch is based on the demand for your product or service. In other words, the price of your product or service changes based on what customers are willing to pay.

Market pricing: This is when you determine your price based on what competitors are charging. You use this type of pricing model if you are selling a product or service that has a competitive market. For example, if you are selling a widget, then you can use market pricing because there are many competitors in the market. But if you are selling a unique product that has no competitors, then you can use variable pricing. If you use market pricing, you will have to determine the average cost of your competitors' products and use that as a benchmark for your pricing.

Moreso; there are many different things that you can do to

enter the market. However, be careful when you are deciding what channel to use. Make sure that you know the competition in that particular market. If you have chosen the wrong channel, it could cost you your entire business. You don't want to take unnecessary risks, do you?

Stage 3: Identify Your Target Market

You need to decide which target market you want to go after. You can choose a market that you know well, or you can choose a market that you know nothing about. Regardless of which option you choose, you need to know that your target market is the right market for you.

The first step in identifying your target market is to understand what kind of product or service you are selling. If you are trying to sell a product or service, you have to find out who your target market is. You can use some tools such as *customer research or focus groups*.

The first step in doing customer research is to gather information about your market. There are many ways to do this, such as talking to people who use your product or services, getting data from the internet, conducting surveys, and interviewing.

Once you gather the information, it is time to analyze it. You can use any analysis techniques you want, but it is important that you identify your target market and its needs.

If you find out what your target market wants, you can then provide them with the type of products or services they need.

You should get to know your target market. Who are they? Where do they live? Where do they work? What do they enjoy?

The people who will buy your products and services are your target market. In other words, they are the people who will purchase your products. If you don't know anything about your target market, you are not going to be able to design a product or service that is perfect for them. If you can't figure out what your target market wants, you are probably going to end up in the same place as everyone else: *not making money.*

What Are Your Target Market's Need?

The first step to becoming successful is identifying your target market. *What are their needs? Why do they need your product or service?*

You must know this before you can start designing a product or service that will solve their problems. If you have no idea about what your target market needs, you might as well just give up and go home.

You might as well just do what everyone else does. There is no way you can succeed in business without knowing your target market's needs.

If you don't know your target market's needs, who does? Your customers.

The people who buy your products or services. They are the ones that tell you what their needs are. It is very easy to find out what your target market's needs are. All you have to do is ask them.

If you want to find out what your target market's needs are, you need to ask them about their problems and the solutions they are looking for, you can also check similar product reviews for better insight. You can ask them directly, or you can get their opinions by checking similar product reviews and asking other people, like your friends, family, co-workers, and even strangers on the street.

You may think that you have a great idea, but it is probably a lot of work to get your product into the market. There are many factors to consider when determining whether or not your product will be successful. For example, if your target market is too small or too big, you won't be able to reach enough people to sell your product. You also need to consider the cost of manufacturing your product. You can't afford to make a product that no one wants. You have to determine the potential demand for your product, then make sure it is affordable for your target market. If you can't meet all of these requirements, your product is probably going to fail.

You also have to make sure that you know how to promote your product effectively. In order to sell your product, you have to create an effective marketing strategy. You have to use different methods of advertising your product to reach your target market. You may have to sell your product through a website, or you may need to have a booth at a local trade show. You may even have to use other methods to get your product noticed by your target market. There are many ways to market your product, but you have to figure out what works best for you.

You will need to think about the following factors when determining how to market your product:

Product Description: Your product description should be clear and concise. Your product description should tell your customers what it does, how it works, and why they should buy it. Your product description should also include all of the features and benefits that your customers will get from buying your product. This is important because if your customers don't know what your product can do, they won't know whether or not they want to buy it. If your product description is too long, your customers might be confused. Your customers may have a hard time understanding all of the details in your product description.

Brand: Your brand is the unique name that you give to your product. You can choose any name that you like, but make sure that your brand is something that your customers recognize.

Target Audience: Your target audience is the group of people who are most likely to buy your product. For example, if you are selling makeup brushes, then your target audience would be women. The more specific your target audience is, the easier it will be for you to reach them with your marketing efforts.

Value: Your value is how much your product is worth to your customers. It is also important to figure out what your competitors offer so that you can see if they are offering a better value than you are.

Why Your Customers Will Buy Your Product: This is an important factor to consider when determining how to market your product. You need to think about why your customers will want to buy your product instead of buying your competitors' products. Why will your customers buy your product? Maybe your customers will buy your product because it is the best quality, or maybe they will buy your product because it is the cheapest. Whatever it is that makes your customers want to buy your product, you need to find out what it is.

How You Will Market Your Product: This is another important part of determining how to market your product.

There are many different ways to market your product. You can advertise your product on the Internet through websites and social media. You can also print advertisements in magazines or newspapers. You can also use marketing techniques such as giving away free samples, providing coupons, and offering discounts. It all depends on what works best for you. The point is that you need to figure out what marketing strategy will be most effective for you.

How Much Money You Will Need to Market Your Product: This is another important factor to consider when determining how to market your product. If you don't have enough money to market your product, then you will have a hard time reaching your target audience. You should estimate how much money you will need to market your product so that you can budget your resources accordingly. When you are trying to determine how to market your product, you will need to consider all of the factors that are listed above. Make sure that you think about everything before you make a decision. Think about the different ways that you can market your product, and choose the one that is the best fit for your product.

Stage 4: How to Make People Buy (17 Success Factors)

To be successful, you need to know how to make people buy. You need to use persuasive techniques to persuade customers.

And you need to use your knowledge of psychology to persuade them in a way that is easy for them to understand. In fact, I'd like to add that the way you speak and write should be tailored to the audience that you are trying to reach. When you write, you should focus on what your audience needs to hear and not what you want to tell them. When you speak, you need to do the same.

This doesn't mean that you need to dumb down your message or make it sound simplistic, but rather that you need to make sure that what you say resonates with your audience's needs.

Now, let me explain. When you are speaking, you need to think about what they need to hear. If you are trying to convince someone of something, you need to make sure that what you are saying is in line with their needs. You need to make sure that it is easy for them to understand. If you can do that, then you will have a much better chance of getting your point across. You need to make sure that your audience understands what you are saying and you need to make sure that they understand it well.

In order to do that, you need to use the right words. When you write, you need to be careful of how you use words because people are much more critical of what they read than they are of what they hear. That is why you need to use the right words in your writing. You need to use the right words because they are going to judge you based on your writing. You need to make sure that your words are simple and easy to understand.

People are much more critical of what they hear than what they read. So, you need to be careful of how you speak.

There are many ways that you can persuade people to buy. You can offer a good deal, give away samples, show your merchandise, or display a product's features.

You need to know the reasons why people buy from you instead of somebody else. It is very important for you to learn these reasons and apply them in your business.

15 Reasons Why People Buy

The most common reason why people buy from you is that

they like your products or services.

The second thing that people like about your business is that it is convenient to probably use and solves a specific problem they have. When people buy your products or services, it is easier for them to do it. It saves their time.

The third reason why people buy from you is that your products or services are better than those of your competitors. Your products or services are more valuable than those of your competitors.

The fourth reason is that your products or services are cheaper than those of your competitors.

The fifth reason why people buy from you is that your products or services are of high quality. When people buy from you, they know that they are getting high-quality.

The sixth reason is that you offer a good value for money. If you are offering your products or services at a price that is lower than that of your competitors, then people will definitely choose you.

The seventh reason is that you have a good reputation. People will buy from you because they know that you are reliable and trustworthy.

The eighth reason why people buy from you is that you offer a guarantee. When people buy from you, they are guaranteed to get what they paid for.

The ninth reason is that you have a good return policy. People will buy from you because they know that you will give them their money back if they are not satisfied with your products or services.

The tenth reason is that you have excellent customer service. People will buy from you because you will make sure that they receive all the answers to any questions they might have about your products or services.

The eleventh reason why people buy from you is that you offer free samples. When people buy from you, they will definitely try your products or services first.

The twelfth reason is that you offer a free trial. When people buy from you, they are given a chance to test out your products or services before they buy them.

The thirteenth reason is that you have a good website. If people can't see how your products or services work, then they won't buy from you.

The fourteenth reason is that you offer a discount. People will buy from you because they know that they will get a discount when they buy from you.

The fifteenth reason why people buy from you is that you offer free delivery. When people buy from you, they are guaranteed to get their products or services delivered at no cost to them.

These factors are what you should work on to ensure your product stays relevant in the market.

Chapter 2

How to Manage Consumer Expectations

Consumers' expectation is one of the most important factors for businesses consideration. When consumers become disappointed with a product, they may give up buying it. To avoid that, you must keep your consumers happy and excited about your product.

The following are tips on how to keep your customers satisfied and excited:

Understand what the customer wants: The first step in keeping your customers happy and excited is to understand what they want. You need to make sure that your product or service meets their expectations. In order to do that, you should conduct research on consumers' needs and expectations.

We should be able to communicate with our customers: This will help us to create an amazing experience for our customers. A good idea is to keep the conversation going after the sale. This is what we call customer service. We should be happy to listen to them, and when they have a problem, we should fix it. As much as possible, we should give a solution to their problems and then walk away. In most cases, this is the best way to do things. If we try to be friendly all the time, our customers will think that we are pushy. This is not a good impression that we want to make. A good customer relationship means that we treat our customers like we would want to be treated if we were in the same situation. Our goal is to have happy customers. This is what we call *customer satisfaction*.

Embrace customer feedback: When working with customers, it is important to find out how satisfied they are with your product or service. Asking them if it is easy for them to use or understand your product is one way to get some feedback. If we don't like something, it's not going to be a positive experience.

Appealing to the people who are your potential customers: This will help to build trust and goodwill for you and your brand. Make sure you use the right tone of voice. In the same way that you would not talk down to someone, don't talk up either. You want to talk to them as if you are talking to a friend. People should be able to relate to what you are saying.

Have a clear goal aside from making money: The goal of a company is to make a positive impact on the lives of people. It's not a good idea for companies to try to make money out of everything. What they are trying to do is to help the people who need the company's products. They want to make a difference in the world. A company needs to take an honest look at itself. It has to figure out what it is and what it is not. The company needs to be clear about what it wants to do.

It needs to have a clear purpose: Once the company figures out what it is and what it is not, then it can focus on what it should be. When building a business, the key to success is to find ways to cut costs. It doesn't matter how much money you are spending on advertising, if you are not making any profit, you will not be successful. If you are running a business, you have to figure out where you can cut costs. You don’t have to make drastic changes to your business. You just need to make some cuts here and there. You can make some minor adjustments to your business and cut costs without having to make big changes.

Be proactive when it comes to marketing: When you are starting a business, you are going to have to spend a lot of time doing research and developing marketing strategies. There is no reason for you to sit back and wait. You should be doing everything possible to market your business. Make sure you are using all of the tools available to you. If you are trying to start a business, you need to take the time to make sure that you know what you are doing. It is going to take a lot of work, and you are going to need to have a lot of patience.

Chapter 3

Creating a Strong Brand

A brand is anything that you are selling. This includes products that are sold at a store. These products could be anything. They could be a product such as a car, a computer, or even a cell phone. It could be something that's created by you or it could be something that you sell such as a business or a product. A brand can be created by a company or an individual. You can also create a brand yourself. Your brand should represent something that people want and will pay for. A good brand has a logo that's memorable. It must also be a name that is easy to pronounce.

In order for a brand to be strong, you need to do a lot of work. The first thing that you need to do is to make sure that you don't just copy other brands. If you do, your brand will not be strong. Instead, you should have your own unique brand.

Also, *your brand is what people will remember when they think of you. It's a reflection of who you are and what you represent.* People will remember you because of the image you project to them. When you think of a brand, you should always try to use adjectives such as *"strong," "powerful," "vital,"* and so on. This will help you to be remembered for a long time.

You should always try to be memorable to the people who are looking at your brand. When you think of your brand, you should try to do things that people will remember about you. It's easy to forget something you have done. But when you create a brand, it will be easy for you to keep in mind what you have done. A brand is not something you can make up. You should make sure that your brand is well-designed. The logo you choose should be unique and clear to the people who are viewing it. Your brand should be something that is attractive to them. You should also make sure that you keep in mind your target audience.

One of the most important factors in building a strong brand is to stand out from others.

Your brand can be anything. It can be your name, a product you offer, your business, your blog, or anything else that defines your business. If you have a strong brand, people will remember your name and come back to you. You should always be unique in your business. There are many businesses in the world, but only a few have a strong brand. You can have the same product or service as another company, but if you have a good brand, people will remember you.

A strong brand is not just a logo. It is a set of values and goals that are shared by all employees in a company and that are communicated through all the activities of the company. For example, **Nike's** tagline says *"Just do it."* It shows what their company is about. The tagline helps to motivate people to do what they want to do. It also encourages them to try harder.

When you have a strong brand, the employees will share the same goals and ideals. They will be more likely to support each other. This makes the company stronger and more competitive. The customers also feel better because they know that the employees are motivated to do what they want to do and what the company stands for.

When you want to create a strong brand, you need to figure out what you want to sell. Think about it. If you are selling a product, then you need to come up with a catchy slogan or a tagline.

Do you want to be the cheapest company out there or do you want to be the best? Think about what you want to do and then you'll know what you want to do. You need to figure out what you want to do. You need to figure out what your main focus will be. *Your values and goals are what determine how strong your brand is.*

The brand of a company represents its *culture, mission, and values.* If the culture of a company is not clear to its customers, then it will not be easy for them to relate to the brand. It will be more difficult for the company to build a relationship with its customers, and as a result, the brand will lose some value. A well-defined brand helps you connect with your customers, and your customers connect with you.

In this chapter, we will discuss:

- The importance of building a strong brand.
- Why a brand is important to your business.
- The three components of a brand.
- The benefits of building a strong brand.

Let's begin by discussing the importance of a strong brand.

How Important is a Strong Brand to Your Business?

If you are looking for short-term results, then your brand may not be as important as other things that you need to focus on, but if you are looking for long-term success, a strong brand can make the difference between success and failure.

In a recent survey of 1,000 business owners, over 70% said that they spent more time and money than they should have on their branding.

That’s why it’s so important to think about what you want your brand to stand for. Let's briefly discuss some tips to help you get started in creating a strong brand for your business.

Know who you are and what you do: The first thing you need to think about when creating a brand is who you are. If you don’t know who you are, how will anyone else? Think about who you are as a business owner. What are your strengths and weaknesses? What are the things that you like doing? What are the things that you don’t like doing? These are all important things to consider.

Next, think about what your company does: What

products or services does your company offer? What makes you unique from other businesses in your industry?

Write down your mission statement: Your mission statement is a short, one-page document that should outline your *vision, values, and core purpose* for your company. It should also be something that you can read every day so that it stays with you.

Think about who your customers are: Think about who your ideal customer is. Who are they? What do they want out of a business? What do they need?

Think about your target market: Think about who your potential customers are. Where do they hang out online? What are their interests? What do they like to read or watch?

Think about your brand identity: This is probably the most important step in the entire process. Once you have an understanding of who you are and what you do, it's time to start thinking about what you want your brand to stand for.

Think about what your brand means: What does your brand mean to you? If you don't know, then it's time to find out. Think about the things that your customers associate with your company. The more you can figure out about your brand, the better.

Develop a strong visual identity: This can be a difficult thing to think about. How do you represent your brand visually? Do you want a logo or a graphic design? How do you want people to see your brand?

Think about your tagline: What is it? Is it catchy? Do people understand it? Does it tell your story?

Think about your colors: This is another important part of branding. Think about your colors. Are they simple and clean? Or are they bold and flashy? What is your overall color palette?

Think about your font: Think about your fonts. Do they look nice? Are they easy to read? Do they work well together?

Think about your logo: Now that you have all of your other branding elements figured out, it's time to think about your logo. You can create a logo in Photoshop or any other graphic design program. Try to make it simple and easy to remember.

Think about your brand message: What does your brand message say? Do you want it to be positive or negative? How do you want your customers to feel when they see your brand?

Create a visual identity for your brand: Once you have all of these pieces figured out, it's time to start building your brand. It may take a while to get everything just right, but once you do, you will have something that is unique and memorable.

Think about what you want to say to your customers: The last step in creating a strong brand is to think about what you want to say to your customers. Think about your brand message. How do you want your customers to feel when they see your brand? Remember, if you don't know, then ask! If you are not sure, then go find out! Once you have all of this figured out, it's time to start thinking about how you can use it to help your business grow.

Why a Brand is Important to Your Business

A brand is one of the most valuable assets a business can own. When it comes to marketing, the ability to stand out and create a unique identity is key. You need to be able to develop a consistent message that your customers will recognize and remember, and that you can use to build relationships with them.

To help you get started on this journey, here are five reasons why brands are important to your business.

A brand is a promise: Your brand represents what you

stand for and what you want to deliver. It's a promise that you make to your customers, both online and offline. It represents who you are and what you're all about, whether you're a local business, an e-commerce company, or an enterprise software provider. When it comes to marketing, a brand can be used as the foundation for all of your other marketing efforts. Your brand provides the foundation from which you launch your marketing campaigns. It also sets the tone for how your audience perceives you and how they respond to your messages. A strong brand is what makes your marketing campaigns effective.

A brand is your voice: The words and phrases that you use in your marketing campaigns are what people will associate with your business. The way you communicate with your audience, and the language that you use help set the tone for how you interact with them. If you want to connect with your customers on a personal level, your messaging needs to reflect this. You need to have a clear and consistent message across all of your marketing channels so that when customers see your ads and hear your message, they know exactly what to expect.

A brand is your identity: Your brand is the overall impression your customers have of your company. It's the idea that they have about you and your business. It's what makes them feel like they know you and they trust you. When it comes to marketing, your brand identity is the face of your business. You can't control how people perceive you, but you can work hard to create a positive identity for your business. That means creating a brand that resonates with your audience and speaks to them on a personal level. Your brand is a reflection of who you are and what you stand for, both online and offline. It's what makes your audience remember you and think about your business when they are looking to buy something or need to make a purchase.

A brand is your customer: Your brand is what you want your customers to think of when they think of you. If they think of you as a local business or an e-commerce site, your brand should reflect that. It should be clear and easy for customers to recognize and associate with you. If they think of you as a provider of enterprise software, then your brand should reflect that too. It's important to have a clear brand identity for your business that makes it easy for your customers to identify with you. Your brand can be used as a tool to create long-term relationships with your customers. When they see your ads, they can associate your brand with a specific message that you want to deliver. Your customers will remember your brand and think about you when they are ready to buy. They will also associate your brand with your company's products or services.

A brand is your reputation: Your brand is the overall impression your customers have of you as a business. It's how they feel about you and your company. It's what makes them trust you and think of you as a reputable business. A strong brand helps your customers identify with your business. It creates a feeling of familiarity and security when they interact with you online or in person. If you want to create long-lasting relationships with your customers, then you need to build a strong brand that they can trust.

Your brand will help your customers feel like they know

you and they can rely on you for the products or services that you offer.

The last point is critical. You want your brand to be something that people want to use and talk about. If you want to develop a brand that is memorable, then it needs to be that people associate with your business. When you use your brand to create a unique identity for your company, then it will be easier for your customers to remember. Your brand should speak to them on a personal level and reflect your business's values. Your brand will be the foundation for everything that you do as a business. If you want to connect with your customers on a personal level, your messaging needs to reflect this. *Your brand provides the foundation for your marketing campaigns. It also sets the tone for how your audience perceives you and how they respond to your messages.*

The Three Components of a Brand.

We live in a world where the concept of a brand is becoming more and more popular. People are buying products with the help of a brand name that they like or trust, and many of them have their own personal brand. When I ask people why they use a certain product, they often tell me that it's because they have heard about it on TV, or because they have read an article about it. And if you think about it, these things do form brands.

There are 3 parts to a brand.

- *A logo*
- *A story*
- *A promise*

The first two of these elements are easy to identify, but the third one is something that we often forget about when creating a brand for ourselves or for others. *The third element is the most important one because, without it, everything else is pointless.* Without a promise, there is no reason to create a brand. If you want your customers to buy from you, you need to give them a reason to buy from you. And this reason can only be found in your promise. A brand is not just a promise. It's a promise that you make to your customers. A promise that you believe in and that you will work hard to deliver on.

So what makes a promise different?

It's what you are going to do when you make it.

A promise has to have a specific action behind it, otherwise, it is just a nice idea that you have. You have to tell your customers what you are going to do, and then you have to keep your promise.

A promise is an action that you want to do, but you need to have confidence in yourself and in your product to make it happen. The first step of the brand-building process is to decide what you want to do. This is the most important part. When you start thinking about this, you should ask yourself some questions:

- What is my brand?
- What does it stand for?
- What is my story?
- What is my promise?
- How can I make my brand different from others?
- What will be my selling points?
- What are the benefits that I can offer my customers?

These are all very important questions to ask yourself, but there is one question that you should also ask yourself, and that is: <u>Why should I do this?</u>

This question is the most important one because it's the foundation of every business. You need to find out why you should do this, and then you need to use that reason to make your brand work.

If you're doing something that you don't really want to do, then why are you doing it? It's not going to work.

If you want to succeed, you have to start with why.

And in order to find this out, you have to ask yourself these questions:

- What do I want to achieve?
- What am I passionate about?
- What are my goals?
- What will I get out of it?
- What is my purpose?
- What does success mean to me?

When you answer these questions, you will see that there is a purpose behind what you want to do. And once you have this purpose, it's time to start creating your brand.

The first step in brand-building is to come up with a *brand name*. ***Brand names*** are important because they are the first thing that people will see when they look at your product or service. A good brand name gives the impression that you are serious about your product, and it also shows that you care about what you are doing. A brand name should be easy to remember and pronounce. If it's too hard to pronounce, then it might not be a good choice.

So how can you come up with a good brand name?

One of the best ways is to make a list of all the words that describe your product or service, and then pick the one that you like the most. It doesn't matter if it's the most common word or not, but it does have to be something that you can use as a brand name. A great example of this is **"Moo"**, which is the brand name of the company that sells beef. Another way is to use the name of your product or service, and then add some extra letters. For example, if your product is called **"The Ultimate Guide"**, then you could use **"theultimateguide.com"** as your brand name.

You can also use the name of your company as your brand name, like ***"theultimateguide"***. If you are having trouble coming up with a good brand name, then you can use a brand name generator by searching online for numerous free services. There are many online tools that can help you come up with a good brand name. Below are some FREE business name generator tool you can use.

namify.tech

namelix.com

businessnamegenerator.com

squadhelp.com/business-name-generator

namesnack.com

The Benefits of Building a Strong Brand.

Your brand is your reputation in the marketplace, and it's the foundation for everything else you do. It's what customers remember when they think about you, and what other people say about you. It's the reason you can have loyal clients who are willing to pay a premium for your services, and the reason that you can charge less for those services than someone who doesn't have a recognizable name.

And it's the reason you can build a strong business on the back of a great reputation. *A strong brand is an advantage.* A strong brand is the basis for any business that makes money. A strong brand builds trust and loyalty with your audience, which results in increased sales and greater customer retention. It's a competitive advantage. Building a strong brand takes time, and requires a significant amount of work. But it’s worth it.

How to Tell a Brand Story that Resonates

Every brand has a story. Every company is in business for a reason. It is not the best product. It's not even the best company. It's about a message that the company wants to send to its consumers. If they don't tell their brand's story, then people may not know who they are. It is important to be able to tell a brand story that resonates with your audience. It is also important to make your audience feel as if they have been personally touched by your brand. The brand story should be told in such a way that it is a unique story that has the potential to make people feel. There are many different ways to tell a brand story. There is no single way to do it. The best brand story will incorporate several different components that have been woven together to make a cohesive story. You want to tell a brand story that makes sense to your target market? Read on.

A Brand Story That Resonates With Your Audience

The best brand stories resonate with your audience and

help them understand what your brand is all about. This helps you build trust and loyalty with your customers.

The most important part of a brand story is its message. You have to think about how people will respond to what you say and the way you say it. In this case, the brand story has to be simple, brief, and meaningful.

Here are some tips for writing your own brand stories.

First, get the message clear. What does the brand stand for? What do you want your customers to know? How do you want them to feel about your brand? What are your core values? What are your unique selling points? What is your brand personality? What is your brand promise? Make sure you know what you want to say and how you want to say it.

Write it down. Now, you have a clear message. You've written down what your brand is all about. Soon, you'll be ready to write a brand story.

Tell a story: Now, you need to tell a story. It's important to tell a brand story that resonates with your audience. Show them what you do. Make sure that your audience can see what you do. How do you make them feel? What do you want them to know? How can you help them?

Tell them why they should buy from you. What makes your brand different from the other brands? How can they trust you?

Keep in mind that you can't just use any old brand story: You need to think about what your audience will like. You need to write a brand story that is relevant to your audience.

Write it down in the form of a story: If you don't write it down, you won't remember it.

Keep it short and simple: If you want to tell a brand story, you should keep it short. It's important to keep it short and to the point. Think about what you want to say and how you want to say it.

Don't be afraid to use numbers: If you want to tell a brand story, you can use numbers. You can say, for example, that you have over 10 million customers. You can also say that your brand has been around for more than 10 years. However, ensure you tell a brand story that is true to you. Think about what your brand is all about. How does your brand want to make a difference? How can your brand make a difference in people's lives?

Don't be afraid to be yourself: If you want to tell a brand story, you should be yourself. Your brand story should be authentic and genuine. If you are afraid of being yourself, you should hire a brand story writer. Immediately, your audience will understand what you're saying.

Keep it positive: Make sure that your brand story is positive. You don't want to use negative words or phrases. You don't want to say that your brand has a lot of problems. If you want to tell a brand story, make sure that it is positive.

Think about what your brand is about: What is the story of your brand? You need to think about how your brand is different from other brands. You need to think about what your brand personality is. *What is your brand promise? What are your brand values?* It's important that you know what your brand stands for. If you don't know, then there's a problem.

Your brand is more than just the logo and the tagline. It's more than a fancy website and it's more than a product or service. It's an entire system that represents everything you do in your business.

That means you should think about how you present yourself to the world.

Chapter 4

Problem Solving Techniques That Works

In this chapter, we shall be discussing in detail, the techniques involved in solving problems, which is the bedrock of any successful business venture.

Identify the Problem

Before you can solve a problem, you have to identify it first. Whether you're an entrepreneur trying to find a business partner, a manager who wants to build better teams, or a boss looking to increase productivity, identifying the problem is one of the most important first steps. In other words, if you don't know what you want, you can't get it.

So what is the problem? Where is the gap between where you are and where you want to be?

To help you identify the problem, start by thinking about what you'd like your customers to be able to accomplish. The next step is to think about the problems your customers encounter while accomplishing those goals.

Finally, think about the problems you've experienced and how you solved them.

To create a *sense of urgency*, identify the problem that needs fixing and what you will do to fix it. If your solution doesn't address the core issue, the urgency won't last and the customer will move on to a competing solution.

Urgency is a powerful selling tool

The easiest way to understand why urgency is a powerful selling tool is to look at what happened after Hurricane Sandy hit the East Coast in October 2012. Consumers who had not planned on buying a home during this period needed to do so quickly because of the threat of losing their homes. They did not have time to shop around for a new place to live, so they went with the first home they came across. After Hurricane Sandy, there was a sense of urgency in housing that consumers could not ignore.

The first step in developing a great product or service is to identify the problem that you can solve. *Your business idea has to be solving a problem. If you don't know what the problem is, how will you ever solve it? You may have a great product, but if it doesn't solve a problem, it won't sell.*

This is important because your product doesn't need to solve every problem in the world. The problem you solve has to be something that your product or service can solve better than what is already available. *Always look out for a unique problem to solve, rather than trying to solve a general or broad problem.*

This is important because the problem you solve has to be a real problem for people.

Take a moment and think about your current business. What problem does it solve? If you can't answer that question, it's probably not a problem worth solving. Ask yourself why people need what you are offering. You need to have a very good answer to that question.

Another great way to determine whether or not you have a real problem to solve is to ask yourself if you are the first to offer this solution.

It's not enough to have a great product. You have to have a great product that solves a problem. ***Sam Amoo***

This is important because it's not enough to have a great product. You have to have a great product that solves a problem. You have to be solving a problem that people are willing to pay you for.

To figure out what problem you can solve, you need to have a clear idea of who your ideal customer is. Your customer will determine the problem you are solving. If you're solving a problem that is unique to you, your ideal customer is you. If you're solving a problem that everyone has, your ideal customer is everyone.

Furthermore, if you can make the product and the solution easier for someone, your ideal customer is that person.

If you're not solving a problem that someone is willing to pay you for, you don't have a business.

If you're not solving a problem that someone is willing to pay you for, you don't have a business.

And you don't have a business until you have a problem you can solve.

It's also important to remember that not every product is a good product. A lot of people think they can start a business selling something that's not a good product.

The problem with this is that it's a bad business.

Furthermore, *if you are solving a problem that is too small, you may have a hard time finding a market for it. If you're solving a problem that is too big, you may have a hard time finding customers for it.*

What do you think your ideal customer is? Is it your mother? Is it your boss? Is it your spouse? Is it your best friend?

Although you may not be able to come up with the answers right away, it will help you get a clearer picture of who your customers are and what you should offer.

The ideal customer for a business is not the person who buys the most products, but rather the person who buys the most products from that business. This is because a business sells to its customers, not to its competitors. The ideal customer for a business is also not the person who has the most money, but rather the person who spends the most money with that business. A business doesn't sell to its competitors, it sells to its customers.

Let's look at the steps involved in identifying and solving a problem.

Analyze the Problem

What do you want to accomplish with this problem? There are two options. You can either do nothing about it or you can try to solve it.

The first thing that you have to do is to analyze the problem. When you are trying to analyze a problem, you should be very careful not to get caught up in the emotions that you feel. In order to analyze the problem, you need to ask yourself why you are experiencing this problem(emphasy on you for now).

Do you think that you have done something wrong? You may have made a mistake or been too careless. Is this something that you didn't plan for? You might have forgotten to prepare for something that you had planned for. It may also be that there was no reason for you to experience this problem. You might have been taken advantage of or there could have been someone else who caused this. In this case, there might be a lot of problems involved.

You should also ask yourself what kind of change you would like to make. What is the best way that you can solve this problem? How much will you pay for the solution? You should always look at the situation realistically. If the price is right and the benefits are great, then go ahead and get it done.

In this part, you need to find out what your product or

service does. You need to define it. It is important to make sure that you have an answer for each question that your customers will ask you. They want to know why they should use your product or service. They also want to know how it can help them in their life.

In this case, you will be able to figure out the main problem your brand wants to solve. You have to remember that your product or service should be very helpful to your target audience. If you're trying to be creative and innovative, you must make sure that the problem your product wants to solve is really important. You will have to consider the most critical problems your audience has. The best way to understand them is to ask people. You can ask people what is troubling them. Also, you can look for people who are struggling to solve their problems.

Your brand should analyze the problems of its target audience.

What is the biggest problem that your brand can solve? How can you help people in their life? That's why it's important to find out what the customer wants to get from your brand. It can be anything you are looking for: *clothing, shoes, bags, gadgets, etc.* You havc to find out what these things are so that you can make them.

You need to think of new and creative ways to help people with their problems. If your brand is an app, you can help people to organize their lives better by giving them helpful hints. This is especially true for products that are trying to improve health. If people are happy with their health, they won't want to buy your product. Therefore, it's important that you listen to the customer's needs and that you try to solve these problems. People will only use your product if they are satisfied with it.

You can know the problem that your brand solves by taking advantage of trends in society. For example, if you were selling shoes, you could market them as a way to make people look good. You can tell people that your products are stylish, fashionable, or that they are cool. You can use these terms to get your customers to think about your product and how they would like to use it. Also, you can use the terms to show how your product makes people feel.

Describe the Problem

One thing that will help you to choose the right type of product is to describe the problem that your potential customers are having. Most people will buy a product if it is solving their problem. The problem that your potential customers are having will be an important factor in determining which product you should offer to them.

You need to think about how your product is going to help solve your potential customer's problems. If you have a product that solves the problem of your potential customers, they'll be more likely to buy it. Also, think about how you can improve upon the solution offered by your competitors. That will help you to create a successful business.

If you can offer a solution that is superior to the solution offered by your competitors, you'll have a competitive advantage

---

Certainly, *if you can offer a solution that is superior to the solution offered by your competitors, you'll have a competitive advantage.*

Once you've defined the problem that your potential customers are having, it's important to consider what features you need to offer in order to solve the problem. The features that you offer in your product will determine what your potential customers will buy.

There are many ways to solve the problem of your

potential customers. You need to consider the features of your product, and how they're going to help solve your potential customer's problems. You can offer the features that your competitors offer, but you need to offer more features.

Look for Root Causes

If you're an entrepreneur, chances are you've had your share of problems. You've likely experienced a brand issue at some point in your life — or in your company's history. Whether it's a product quality issue, customer service breakdown, or a marketing campaign that doesn't connect with the market, you're bound to encounter problems. So how can you identify root causes? You should start with a broad, external assessment.

The first step in problem-solving is to figure out what's causing the problem. Are you having a problem with your product, or are you having a problem with your customers? Maybe your product is performing better than expected, but your customers aren't buying. Is your company's marketing message not resonating with your target market? Or maybe you're getting feedback from your customers that you don't understand.

Here are a few suggestions:

1. Conduct a Survey

Surveys are great for uncovering problems. But they're also great for identifying root causes, too.

You should make it a habit to find out the root cause of the problem. If you don't know the root cause, you'll not be able to come up with the right solution. By making a decision about the root cause, you will be able to create a good solution. As an example, *take this one from a restaurant franchise owner who was experiencing low sales. They found out that a lot of people are looking for restaurants that are convenient, but they don't want to spend much money. They then discovered that they were selling their food at an expensive price. That made sense because they wanted to attract more customers.*

Many companies complain that they have a problem that keeps them from increasing sales. However, *their top priority is to solve the wrong problem.* What they need to do is to take a step back to examine the true problem that is keeping sales down. *They should focus on what is happening and not on what they can't do or what the competition is doing.*

> *Focus on what is happening and not on what you can't do or what the competition is doing.*

"What's your biggest problem?" is a simple question, but it can yield surprising results. For example, you might be surprised to learn that your biggest problem isn't actually your product or service, but rather a lack of demand. In other words, you're underselling your products or services. *What do you think is your biggest problem? And how can you use that information to identify root causes and solutions?*

What is the one thing that is the most important for your business to change? I've been thinking a lot about this. The one thing that I'm going to say is that it's not the money you are not making. *It's not about the amount of money you are not making in business. It's about the attitude. It's about the way that you feel about your business and your perspective on what is happening around you and your business.*

2. Collect Data

Once you've identified your biggest problem, it's time to collect data.

There are two important questions to ask when you're looking for data: *What data should you collect? What data will be most useful to you?* For example, you might collect data on your sales, profits, or leads. You might collect data on your competitors. You might collect data on your customers. You might collect data on your product or service.

The key to collecting data is to identify the most relevant and actionable data.

Once you've collected the data, you need to analyze it. **Data analysis** is an essential step of your business and ***marketing analytics process.*** It's about understanding what the data tells you and using that information to guide future decisions.

If you know why your customer chose one option over another, then you can decide what you want to do next. For example, if you found that your sales increased because you increased your prices, then you could try to increase your prices again to see if that increases sales.

Once you know what to do, it's time to implement the

strategy.

The next step is **implementation.** The best way to implement a new strategy is by testing it out before rolling it out to a larger audience. You can use the data from your marketing analytics to help guide your testing.

A test is often called a *"dry run"* or *"shakedown cruise"*. For example, you might test your strategy with just five people to see if it works as you expect it to. If it doesn't, you can decide whether you need to make adjustments to it or whether you need to scrap it.

What if you find out that your new strategy doesn't work?

There are two ways to fix an unsuccessful strategy. *You can modify the strategy or replace it.*

If you decide that your new strategy needs to be modified, then you have to determine what changes you want to make. Sometimes, when you make a change, it's not the best solution. For example, you could try to raise prices again if it didn't increase your sales.

If you decide that the new strategy isn't the best one, you could choose to scrap it and go back to the old strategy. Or you could use the data to identify other options that could work.

The other option is to replace the strategy with a new one. You can do this by changing your marketing strategy or by changing your product or service. For example, if your strategy didn't work, then you could change the way you advertise or the way you offer your products or services.

You can also use data analytics to identify which strategies are working. For example, if you found that you were able to sell more products by offering a free gift, then you could offer free gifts to all of your customers.

You can also use data analytics to help you choose the right marketing strategy. For example, if you found that the best way to increase sales was to offer a special discount to your best customers, then you could give that discount to your best customers.

The most important thing to remember is that the purpose of data analytics is to help you make better decisions.

The purpose of data analytics is to help you make better decisions

---

3. Solve the problem

Once you've uncovered your biggest problem, the next step is to solve it.

What can you do to address it? Can you add a new feature? Improve the user experience? Reduce your price? Change your marketing strategy? How do you know if you're solving the problem?

One of the ways that you can determine if you've solved your problem is by looking at the number of inquiries (or users) that you're receiving. Do you have fewer requests than you did in the past? If so, congratulations. You've probably made the problem more visible to potential customers and more accessible.

If you see fewer inquiries than you did previously, don't think of this as a bad thing. It could mean that your product or service is meeting a need of people who were searching for it in the past, but who don't need it anymore. That's a very valuable insight!

Another way to determine whether or not you've solved your problem is to look at how many users you're getting. Is the number of inquiries that you're getting higher or lower than you did in the past? If it's higher, then you may have added something new to the problem and created a new need for customers. On the other hand, if the number of inquiries is lower, you may have solved the problem.

If you're getting more or less inquiries than you were

getting before, there's no need to be alarmed. It could also means that more customers are finding the product or service through other channels and are not using your platform to make inquiries. This might mean that your product has lost some appeal to potential customers and that you'll need to re-evaluate whether it makes sense for your business to continue using the strategy used.

However, don't worry too much about this—it's perfectly fine. If you find that more inquiries are coming in from other channels, that's an excellent sign that you have a great product that is valuable to customers from that channel.

If you're getting fewer inquiries than before, that's cause for concern. It could mean that your product or service isn't providing value to people who are looking for it, or it could mean that you aren't offering the best value for your services. Either way, you should definitely be concerned and you may need to evaluate whether you can continue to use the strategy if the problem persists.

If you're not getting any inquiries at all, that's even worse! You should definitely start evaluating why your product or service isn't being found by potential customers. You may have some competition that is doing a better job of marketing and promoting their product, or you might have a problem with your own product or service. Regardless, it's important to know what the reason is so you can improve your marketing efforts.

You may need to work harder to promote your product and get more people to use your product and services.

Develop Alternate Solutions

As a brand, you're not selling yourself any more than a company is. Your customers are the ones selling your brand. If you have an idea for a product or service, you should use every tool at your disposal to develop alternate ways to sell the brand.

Once you've determined the primary goals of your sales message, the next step is to develop alternate solutions to these goals. When you're looking for ways to increase the effectiveness of the main sales message, the first thing to do is to get in front of potential customers. Ask yourself these questions: What if I were to use another piece of software to accomplish the same thing? How would I do it differently, and why should I?

If you want to become the preferred brand choice of consumers, you need to offer consumers a unique value proposition. One of the easiest ways to accomplish this is to come up with alternate solutions to a consumer problem. Once a problem is identified, you'll need to think about how other products or services can solve that problem in a different way. Then, you'll need to figure out how you will communicate that alternative solution to your audience.

You should be creative in solving consumer problems. You can think of new ways of solving these problems. It is not enough to be simply original or have good ideas. You need to use them and show the consumer that your product or service is better than those already on the market. Consumers are smart, so they should be able to tell when they are getting a good deal. They should know the differences between your product or service and the products and services that are already available. *Don't be afraid to share your alternate solutions.*

This is a very important part of developing alternate solutions. Consumers will always be looking for the best way to solve a problem. If you can solve the problem in a way that is different from the others, you will have an edge over your competitors. It's important to think about the problems that your target audience faces and come up with a solution to them. If you're looking to sell more than one product or service, you should look at your target audience and come up with alternate solutions to their problems.

If you can solve the problem in a way that is different from the others, you will have an edge over your competitors.

You need to be creative when coming up with solutions to consumer problems. Consumers are looking for ways to solve their problems and they are looking for the best way to do it. It is important that you think about how your brand can help consumers solve their problems. You need to make sure that your brand is in front of your audience and that they are aware of the solutions that your brand can offer them. If you don't think about your brand's place in the market, you will not be able to solve consumer problems.

You should identify the problems that your audience is having. You should also identify the problems that your audience is not having. Then, you should brainstorm as many ideas as you can to solve the problems.

You can then consider how you can market your business and improve your marketing efforts so that you can get more inquiries through your platform. For example, if you sell shoes on Amazon, you can use the Merchant Center to promote your shoe sale. You could write a blog post about your shoes or create a video to share with the world about how great your shoes are. You could even run a contest where you give away a pair of shoes to someone who comments on your blog post or shares your video. The possibilities are endless!

Implement the Solution

This step is one of the more time-consuming parts of the research process, but if done right, it will yield valuable results. The first thing to do is list out the findings of the survey, either on a spreadsheet or word document. The second part is figuring out what you can do to solve these problems. Listing them out will help you identify gaps, opportunities, and solutions, and make it easier to pinpoint which solutions are the most effective. This is where the brainstorming begins.

Take a look at the top 10 results from the survey you ran earlier, and implement the solution (product, service, etc.) that you think is going to be most impactful. You can use whatever tool you want to accomplish this (e.g., Google Analytics, Google Sheet, Trello, etc.). For example, if your top two results are "product" and "service," the solutions for these results would be *"increase customer retention,"* and *"increase sales,"* respectively.

Once you identify these solutions, go through each one and write out what you will do to achieve the solution.

This means that you need to find the solution that is most likely to increase the number of people that participated in your survey. The solutions for this are:- *"Increase customer retention," "Increase sales," and "Decrease bounce rate"*

Once you identify these solutions, you can start implementing them. For example, if the solution for the "Increase sales" solution is to "increase customer retention," then you can start working on the "increase customer retention" solution. Once you have implemented this solution, you can make changes to that particular solution. You might want to increase the amount of information or content that you share with the users, as this would be a possible solution. You could also consider a new solution that would increase customer retention. This might be something like adding a discount or coupon code. Another solution might be a different design for the landing page.

A good way to improve your landing pages is to work on the elements that don't perform very well. The most important thing is to analyze where the problem lies and figure out what the solution is. Once you have identified the solution to the problem, implement it.

Keep doing this until the problem stops occurring. It's also important to keep an eye on the metrics that you have set up.

It's up to you now to implement your solutions. It might take some time before you start seeing the results, but it won't take long for you to see a difference in your business. However, there are things that you need to keep in mind when you implement your solutions.

First, *you should always use effective tactics. Make sure that you don't put everything in one bucket. You should use multiple strategies and solutions.* Then you need to focus on each of these strategies or solutions. Your goal is to help users. So you have to make sure that you provide relevant information that is important to them.

You also need to think about what is going to motivate them to continue using your product or service.

If you do this, you will achieve success. Once you are

finished with the implementation, you need to monitor whether it is working. It might take some time for your users to start noticing the changes you are making, but you should definitely see positive results after you implement your strategies and solutions.

Absolutely, you can see results after you implement your solutions. In fact, you will start seeing results right away. But you should always keep in mind that you need to continue with your strategies and solutions. You need to continue making improvements. This is the only way that you can make sure that your product or service will continue to provide the best user experience possible.

There are many ways to help you implement your strategies and solutions. However, you need to make sure that you have a clear plan in mind. You need to make sure that you have a clear vision of what you want to achieve. You also need to make sure that you have a clear understanding of the problems that you are trying to solve. Then you can start working on your strategies and solutions.

Measure the Results

As mentioned earlier, the first thing you want to do when you've gathered feedback is to measure the results of your survey. How many of the survey respondents clicked through? Did the most recent conversion rate go up or down? If you found something interesting in the survey, then use this feedback to create a more relevant landing page or product that can make it easier for users to buy your product.

A key component of gathering feedback and creating a product that customers will want is having a way to measure the results of your surveys and other research.
The results of the survey can be used to determine which changes in messaging or offer can increase conversion. Use the most effective wording for each response to make sure your conversions stay high. In addition, this data can be used to improve future surveys and emails to customers. You may also decide to alter the way you contact those who did not respond positively. The most important thing here is to keep asking until you get a positive response from your customers.

Repetition and Consistency

Your audience must understand and feel like they've been there before and gotten what they want from you. If it's not the same product or service your audience has already seen or heard, chances are they won't remember it. If you're trying to persuade the listener to buy something, the first step is to make sure they are aware of what they're being persuaded to buy. And then make sure they know how you can deliver it. *The next step is to remind them of what they already know and make sure they know it in a new way or with new information.*

Repetition *is a powerful sales tool that doesn't always have to be done word for word.* For example, a brand can use a unique hook in an ad to grab attention, then use that same message to drive their home page or social media pages.

When it comes to selling, repetition is a critical aspect.

If you don't believe that, let me ask you this: *If you want your customers to think of you when they're looking for your product or service, how many times do you want to be at the forefront of their minds?*

The answer will reveal the importance of repetition. For example, if we want to get people to think of us when they're searching for a restaurant, we probably wouldn't need to mention it a few times. We just want people to remember that we exist, which means we only need one chance to make an impression.

Consistency is a powerful way to influence consumers. It works because it gives people a sense of what is expected and what they can expect if they follow a path. Once they've developed a sense of familiarity and comfort with a brand or a product, it becomes easier to go with it. And if it's consistently good, there will be less need to seek out other options.

Repetition and consistency for products and services are other of the most powerful tools that can help sell like a titan

---

Repetition and consistency for products and services are other of the most powerful tools that can help sell like a titan. For example, if you own a dog, you probably want to do anything you can to keep him/her out of trouble. So, it's in your best interest to teach your dog to sit when he comes to the door. You do this by repeating the same behavior until the dog starts to pick up on the fact that he is going to receive some kind of positive reinforcement when he sits.

Summing up, you want to make sure your audience knows that you are a reliable company and that they can trust you to do what you say you will do. You also want to make sure that your audience knows what they can expect from you. In the case of the dog example, your audience needs to know that they can expect to see a dog sit at the door when they come to visit. If they are consistently seeing a dog that doesn't sit, it's going to be more difficult to teach the dog to sit. So, consistency is a powerful tool that can help sell.

So, what does this all mean? *When you're selling, repetition is one of the most important tools you can use*. The more times you repeat a message, the more likely your audience is to remember it, which is why you should not limit your business marketing and promotion to one channel, or a particular time.

Chapter 5

The Psychology of Marketing

Psychology is the study of the human mind and behavior. It is an interdisciplinary science that focuses on *cognition, emotion, motivation, personality, behavior, social behavior, mental disorders, and many other topics*. The study of psychology is often confused with the study of psychiatry. While they are related, there are clear differences between them.

Psychology is a social science that focuses on the understanding of human behavior. Psychology is one of the oldest sciences. It was born with the birth of mankind. It was not until the late 1800s that psychologists began to use scientific methods to better understand human behavior.

In the 1900s, psychology began to focus more on how to help people in their everyday lives. In the beginning, psychology was more about studying the nature of man. Today, psychologists are still interested in the nature of man. They are still trying to understand what makes us tick. However, psychologists are also interested in how we can improve our society and culture. For example, if we have an issue with violence, then psychologists will try to figure out what is causing it and how we can prevent it.

Psychology is not just for kids. Although children are often the first ones to be studied, psychologists are interested in all people. People of any age can benefit from psychology. Psychologists are interested in helping people who have problems in their everyday lives. They may help people with learning disabilities, mental illnesses, physical disabilities, or other problems. They may also help people who have personality disorders, mental health issues, or other problems.

Psychology is a science that is constantly evolving. New research is always being done. Psychology is very broad. It covers many different topics. However, psychology does share some commonalities.

In marketing, psychology is used to help explain why people behave the way they do. We're all human beings with a shared set of emotions and feelings. We also share the same needs and desires as well as the same frustrations when things don't go our way. So why are we so different from one another? *Well, part of that answer lies in the psychology of our brains.*

We each have a brain that has been designed for survival. It's an organ that's responsible for keeping us alive by filtering out all the information we don't need. This can cause it to become a bit of a filter bubble, where we only see what we want to see and ignore all the rest. But that's okay. That's how it's designed. But sometimes we need to look beyond that. We need to step outside of our own brains and look at the world around us. It might be difficult at first, but if we keep at it long enough, we'll start to notice patterns in the data we're looking at and make sense of it. We can use that knowledge to help us make decisions or even just understand ourselves better.

If you want to sell more like titans, you need to understand your customers, what motivates them, and how their minds work.

If you want to sell more like titans, you need to understand your customers and how their minds work. You need to know what motivates them, what excites them, and what they're looking for. *The key to selling more is to figure out what your audience wants before you ask them for it.*

There are two ways to approach the process of selling more: *Determine your customers' needs first, then offer them the solution that will meet those needs.* Or, *determine what the customer wants, then offer them a solution that gives them what they want.* Selling more isn't as easy as it sounds.

To begin with, it's not always clear what you're trying to sell and who you're selling it to. If you're looking to sell more, you'll have to make sure that you know what you're selling, how you're going to sell it, and who's going to buy it.

As you are probably aware, psychology has a lot to do with marketing. Let's take a look at the most important things that you need to know about psychology and marketing.

What is Marketing Psychology?

Psychology is the study of how people think and act. When marketers talk about psychology, they are talking about the mental processes of consumers. This includes how people make decisions and how they behave in certain situations. When we look at marketing, we can see that it is a form of psychological communication. When we market products or services, we want our audience to believe that we are trustworthy and reliable.

If you've ever been to an airport, you know that there are always several people waiting in line for the security checkpoint. If you are traveling alone, you might be worried about standing in a long line, but if you are traveling with friends or family, you'll probably be able to wait in line for hours together. The reason why we can all stand in the same line together is that we have a shared set of expectations. If one person is ahead of the line, then the next person knows that they will eventually be able to get through. In the same way, we expect that marketing will work the same way. When you are planning your marketing strategy, it is important to consider what your audience expects from your brand. This means that you need to know the beliefs and values of your target audience. It is also important to understand how your customers think and act in certain situations. If you don't understand your audience, then you will struggle to create marketing strategies that are relevant and effective.

In this chapter, we'll look at how marketing psychology can help you market more effectively.

Understanding Human Behavior

Before you can understand how your audience thinks, it is

important to understand human behavior. Marketing psychology helps us understand the psychological processes that drive our decisions and behaviors. It also helps us predict how people will behave in certain situations. If you are planning to run a business, then you need to understand how people think. When you are running a business, you need to make sure that you are aware of the psychology behind your products or services. This way, you can plan marketing campaigns that are relevant and effective.

There are several different approaches that you can use to understand human behavior. One of the most popular ways of understanding human behavior is through *cognitive psychology*. This type of psychology looks at how our brain works. When we are learning about human behavior, we should try to look at how our brains work. A lot of what we know about human behavior comes from studying the brain. Brain research has helped us understand the psychology behind our decision-making. *Cognitive psychology* helps us understand the role that our beliefs and values play in our decision-making. When we make decisions, we use all of our senses to process information. We rely on our eyes and ears to gather information about the world around us. When it comes to marketing, we often rely on visual and auditory cues to help us make decisions.

However, it is important to remember that our brains are more than just our sensory organs. *Our brains also have an emotional component. We can't separate our emotions from our beliefs and values.* Our brains are constantly processing information. This means that we are always making decisions and changing our minds. This is why we need to understand how our brains work when it comes to marketing. The best way to understand how our brains work is to study cognitive psychology.

Cognitive Psychology

Before you can understand how people think, you first need to understand how your brain works. Cognitive psychology is a branch of psychology that studies how our brain works. In this section, we'll look at the different parts of the brain and how they affect decision-making. The brain has two main parts: *the brainstem and the cerebral cortex*.

When we think about our brain, thc ***brainstem*** comes to mind first. The *brainstem* is responsible for basic functions such as breathing and regulating our heartbeat. It also deals with reflexes. When we make a decision, the *brainstem* helps us to process information that we gather through our senses. It is also responsible for emotions and instincts.

The ***cerebral cortex*** is the most complex part of the brain. *It is responsible for the more advanced functions such as thinking, reasoning, problem-solving, and creativity.* We often think about the cerebral cortex when we think about our brain because it is responsible for our conscious thoughts. However, our brains are constantly processing information in the background. We don't even have to be thinking about something to process information. The brain has three main areas: *the prefrontal cortex, the limbic system, and the paralimbic cortex.*

The *prefrontal cortex* is responsible for higher-level cognitive functions such as planning, decision-making, and problem-solving. The *limbic system* is responsible for our emotions and instincts. The *paralimbic cortex* is responsible for our emotions. This means that we can't separate our emotions from our beliefs and values. These different parts of the brain work together to help us make decisions and understand human behavior.

Cognitive Psychology of Marketing

Now that we know how our brains work, let's look at how cognitive psychology applies to marketing. In this section, we'll discuss the different parts of the brain with respect to marketing, how they affect decision-making, and what we can learn from cognitive psychology.

Brainstem: The brainstem is responsible for basic functions such as breathing and regulating our heartbeat. It also deals with reflexes. When we make a decision, the brainstem helps us to process information that we gather through our senses. It is also responsible for emotions and instincts. The brainstem has two major functions:

1. **Sensory Integration:** The brainstem gathers information from our senses and processes it so that we can make decisions. For example, if we see something, smell something, or hear something, our brainstem integrates the information that we are gathering into a single experience. This means that we don't have to think about how many things we are sensing at one time.
2. **Emotion and Instincts:** The brainstem also helps us to feel emotions and instincts. We often think about the

brainstem when we think about our brain because it is responsible for our emotions and instincts. However, the brainstem also helps us to process information in the background. We don't even have to be thinking about something to process information.

Our brainstem processes this information so that we can make decisions.

Prefrontal Cortex: The *prefrontal cortex (PFC)* is the newest part of the brain. It was not discovered until the mid-1800s, and scientists are still working to understand how it works. It is also one of the most important parts of the brain. It is responsible for decision-making, planning, and reasoning. It is also the area where you process language and symbols. The **PFC** is very flexible. It can be trained to think differently than it normally does. For example, if we practice the art of mindfulness, we will become more aware of things that are happening around us. If we practice meditation, we will learn to calm down and become less reactive. This section is a great example of how cognitive psychology can help us to learn more about ourselves. We can look at our brains and see how they affect our decisions. We can also use this knowledge to better understand our behavior and make better decisions. If we look at our brain, we can see that there are different areas of the brain that are responsible for different types of decisions. This helps us to understand why we make some of the decisions that we do. For example, when we are looking at a website, we are using the visual cortex of our brain. We can see the pictures and videos on the website, but the text is not important to us. We are not reading what the website has to say, we are only looking at the pictures. The prefrontal cortex, which is responsible for reasoning and decision-making, is not activated in this type of situation. We have learned that we don't need to read text when we are just looking at pictures. In other situations, we will be looking at a website that has text on it. We will also be using our prefrontal cortex. It will help us to understand what the website has to say. The prefrontal cortex is also responsible for how we make decisions. When we are making decisions, the prefrontal cortex helps us to plan and consider all of the options before we make a decision. For example, if we are deciding between two jobs, the prefrontal cortex helps us to think about what the job entails. It will help us to decide which job is better. It is also important to note that the prefrontal cortex is responsible for more than just decision-making. It is also responsible for reasoning. This means that it helps us to figure out why things happen. The prefrontal cortex helps us to make sense of things that happen around us. It helps us to understand how things work and why things happen.

Cognitive psychology is applied in marketing to help us understand how people think, and what they are looking for when they shop. It also helps us develop marketing strategies that will help our clients and customers.

How Cognitive Psychology can Help us Sell more products?

Cognitive psychology is the study of how our minds work and what makes us tick. You might know that our brains have evolved to help us survive in a world full of predators, but you may not know that our brains are also wired to be helpful to us when we want to sell something to someone else. When it comes to selling, cognitive psychology can help you understand why people buy your product and how you can make them buy more.

Cognitive psychologists look at the human brain as a "thinking" machine. We are constantly making decisions about what we think about and how we should act in different situations. Cognitive psychologists call these decisions *"cognitive processes."* These processes happen at an unconscious level, so most people are not even aware that they are making these decisions. You have probably made many of these decisions yourself without even realizing it. When you go to a store, you are automatically guided by your unconscious mind to pick up a certain kind of shoe, or maybe you would like to buy a certain brand because you've always had good luck with it. It doesn't matter whether you realize this or not, you have made a choice based on your past experiences. The same thing happens when you are trying to sell something to someone else. Cognitive psychologists have found that when you try to sell something, your brain is trying to make decisions about whether or not the person will buy your product. If the person does not like what you are selling, then your brain will automatically make decisions to stop you from selling it to them.

Cognitive psychologists have found that your brain has several different *"decision-making processes."* When you are deciding whether or not to buy a particular product, your brain is making decisions about:

What you think about the product. For example, do you think the product is useful? Will it help you make money? Does it look nice?

How much you like the product. Do you like the way it feels in your hands? Do you like the colors? Do you like how it sounds?

What you think about the person who is buying the product. For example, are you afraid of the person who is going to buy your product? Do you think they will be fair? Will they pay you back? Do you think they are honest?

What you think about yourself. For example, are you thinking that you are not good at selling things? Are you thinking that you don't have enough time? Do you feel like you're going to be embarrassed if you try to sell something?

You can think of these decision-making processes as *"cognitive biases"* or *"mental shortcuts."* For example, you might think that you do not have enough time to spend selling something when you really do have time to do it. Or maybe you feel that you are not good at selling things when you actually are good at it.

These biases cause you to make decisions that are not in

your best interest. They also happen so quickly that you don't realize you are making them until after the fact. That's why cognitive psychologists call them *mental shortcuts or biases*. The brain is always trying to make decisions for us. In most cases, our brains are automatically trying to make the best decisions for us.

The problem is that sometimes we don't realize that we are making decisions based on our past experiences and our biases. We need to learn how to overcome these automatic decisions in order to sell more products. When you are trying to sell something to someone else, you can use these cognitive biases to your advantage. When you are trying to sell a product to someone, you should make sure that you are thinking about:

- What you want to get out of this product.
- What the other person wants.
- The product itself.
- Your own personal interests.
- How you are going to sell it.

Once you have all of this information, you should be able to make better decisions about whether or not to sell something to someone else.

Let's take a look at some examples of cognitive biases that

you might use when you are trying to sell a product.

Decision-making bias #1: ***The Availability Bias:*** This is a cognitive bias where you are more likely to think that you have a good idea because you have seen it more often than you do because it is true. For example, if you are thinking about selling a product that costs $50, and you think about all of the products that cost $50, you will only think about the ones that you have seen before. You are more likely to think about the products that you have seen, even though you know that they are not good ideas.

Decision-making bias #2: ***The Representativeness Bias:*** This is a cognitive bias where you are more likely to think that something is true because it is similar to something that you have seen before. For example, if you are trying to sell a product to someone else, you will be more likely to think that the product is going to be good if you have seen a similar product before. You might have seen a product like this one in a catalog. You know what to expect from the product, and you know what it looks like. This means that when you see a similar product, you will think that it is going to be good.

Decision-making bias #3: ***The Anchoring Bias:*** This is a cognitive bias where you are more likely to think that something is true because it is close to what you think about first. In other words, you are more likely to think that something is true if you have just thought about it before. For example, if you are trying to sell a product to someone else, you might think that the product is going to be good because you just thought about the product. You might have just read about the product in a magazine or newspaper. This means that when you read about a product, you might think that it is going to be good

Why is Cognitive Psychology Used in Marketing?

I've always found cognitive psychology fascinating, and I've always wondered why marketing research is so often driven by it. So I'm interested to see if there are any specific reasons why this is the case. Here are my top five reasons:

It helps explain human behavior: In psychology, we know that the way people process information is different from the way computers do it, so we can understand why they behave the way they do. If you want to get them to buy something, for example, you have to understand what motivates them and how you can appeal to their motivations.

It gives us a common language: In psychology, we talk about motivation, learning, and attention as "processes" (rather than "things"). This makes it easier to understand one another when we're talking about these things, which means that we don't have to use fancy scientific jargon. It also makes it easy to understand the research results, because the processes are so familiar to us.

It provides a framework for designing experiments: In psychology, we usually design experiments using a theory of how people learn, rather than just trying to figure out what the results of an experiment will be. This helps us figure out which experiments will work best for a particular goal, and we can design those experiments more efficiently.

It gives us a way to talk about the real world: If you know something about how people think, you can design experiments that are more likely to yield useful results. For example, if you know that people like to compare products, you can design an experiment where you ask people to compare two products, instead of asking them to rate one product on a scale.

It helps us avoid common mistakes: In psychology, we have a lot of experience with people's cognitive limitations, so we know where they're going to make mistakes when designing experiments. This makes it easier to avoid those mistakes, which means that we can design experiments more efficiently.

Understanding Your Customers

You cannot succeed in marketing without knowing your customers. The more you understand your customers, the more you can do to help them and the more effective your marketing will be. Your customers are different. They are people with different personalities, backgrounds, beliefs, and values. If you don't know your customers, you cannot design a marketing campaign that will work for them.

As you learn more about your customers, you will be able to figure out what motivates them. If you know their motives, you can design marketing campaigns that will help them achieve their goals.

12 Psychological Bases that Drive Customer Behavior

As you are probably aware, psychology is the study of the human mind and behavior. In marketing, psychology is used to help explain why people behave the way they do. If you want to sell more, you need to understand your customers and how their minds work.

There are 12 basic psychological principles that drive

customer behavior. They are as follows:

1. The customer's feelings.
2. The customer's needs.
3. The customer's desires.
4. The customer's perceptions.
5. The customer's motivations.
6. The customer's goals.
7. The customer's perceptions of value.
8. The customer's perceptions of risk.
9. The customer's attitudes.
10. The customer's feelings about the product.
11. The customer's expectations.
12. The customer's emotions.

Chapter 6

The Psychology of Motivation

Most of the research around the psychology of motivation deals with the *"push"* side of motivation. ***Push strategies*** involve external factors that make us feel the need to change. For example, the desire to lose weight, gain a promotion or pay off debt. While these motivations are important and necessary for change, a shift toward motivation by its nature can often lead to resistance. It's harder to stick to our goals if we are feeling stressed or angry. On the flip side of motivation, there are internal or *"pull" strategies.* ***Pull strategies*** rely on internal motivation and are rooted in values or goals.

In fact, some of the most persuasive online ads are those that exploit our motivation to feel like we're doing something good for others. When you're writing copy for a donation, it makes sense to talk about the good deeds you've done in the past and the ways you've helped people. It's also a great idea to mention the benefits you'll receive as a result of your purchase—whether it's a tax write-off, a charitable deduction, or an increase in customer loyalty.

The second psychological principle that marketers and entrepreneurs should know about is ***motivation***. We, humans, are motivated to do things, and what we do can be motivated by one of two basic psychological principles: *intrinsic motivation or extrinsic motivation.*

Intrinsic motivation is an internal motivation to act, whereas **extrinsic motivation** is a desire to act in the service of something else. Both are important to understand and utilize.

According to motivation theory, there are three basic ways that people can be motivated: *intrinsically, extrinsically, and socially.*

Intrinsic motivation is motivated by things like the feeling of accomplishing a task or reaching a goal.

Extrinsic motivation is motivated by external rewards, such as money, prizes, or trophies. While this type of motivation is often seen in the context of business.

Social motivation is a more common type of extrinsic motivation. *Extrinsic motivators* tend to create a short-term, one-time response to a need or desire. The most common of these types of motivators are *money and prizes*. However, it's important to remember that external motivators are not a good long-term solution because they do not last. In order to make lasting, sustainable changes, individuals need to be intrinsically motivated.

In order to make lasting, sustainable changes, individuals need to be intrinsically motivated.

Whereas extrinsic motivators are often short-term solutions, intrinsic motivators are long-term solutions.

One of the main differences between *intrinsic and extrinsic motivation* is that intrinsic motivation requires an individual to want to do something. Intrinsic motivation comes from an individual's desire to engage in an activity, while extrinsic motivation comes from an external motivator. An individual's intrinsic motivation can come from any number of factors, but it is the most common factor in a person's desire to do something.

An example of intrinsic motivation is when you wake up and want to go for a run. If you have to force yourself to go for a run, then you are probably not intrinsically motivated to go for a run. On the other hand, if you are intrinsically motivated to go for a run, then you are likely to go even if you don't have to force yourself to do so. In addition, intrinsic motivation comes from a person's interest in an activity, not from a person's interest in the outcome of the activity.

Whereas extrinsic motivators often create a short-term response, intrinsic motivators can create long-term, sustainable changes.

There are four main ways that intrinsic motivation can be created:

Cognitive – this type of motivation is created when a person thinks about the task or activity and the feeling of doing it. For example, if a person has to take care of an elderly relative, he or she will be motivated by the cognitive aspect: taking care of someone and being helpful and kind.

Affective – this type of motivation is created when a person feels the feelings of doing something. It can be created through positive reinforcement, such as praise and rewards, or negative reinforcement, like removing something that makes you feel bad (e.g., being yelled at by your boss).

Volitional – this type of motivation is created when a person wants to do something and then does it.

Involuntary – this type of motivation is created when a person does not want to do something but then does it anyway.

When creating intrinsic motivation, it is important to think about the task or activity itself. It's not enough to think about the feeling of doing it. You also need to think about the activity itself.

Chapter 7

The Psychology of Persuasion

This psychology principle is probably the easiest one to explain. When we persuade someone, we try to make them believe what we believe. In other words, we tell a story about the world that convinces others that our beliefs are true. If we want a person to buy something, we try to convince them to see it as the best thing they could buy right now.

We also convince people to do things because of what we think will happen to them if they don't. We persuade them because we want them to act in the way we want them to. The only reason you should be concerned with this is if you're in the persuasion business.

Persuasion is a useful tool for persuading others to believe your ideas. But if you're selling products or services, your goal isn't necessarily to convince the person who's buying them to buy them. You're trying to sell them on the idea that they need to buy your product or service. If you can convince someone that they need your product or service, then you've succeeded. In addition to influencing people, we also use our minds to solve problems.

Here's an example of how we solve problems. You have a problem and you want to solve it. So, you sit down and think about the problem. You consider all the things that could go wrong and figure out a solution for each one. Eventually, you come up with a solution that fixes the problem. If you're not good at solving problems, you might find yourself thinking about ways to avoid having the problem.

We also solve problems by reasoning from what we know about the world to what we believe is true. For example, if I believe that the sky is blue and you believe that the sky is green, then I'm going to be able to reason about the color of the sky better than you can. It's easier to reason about the color of the sky than it is to actually look at the sky.

We also use our minds to remember things. We remember things by thinking about them. For example, if I want to remember the fact that the sky is blue, I might think about the sky. If I remember the color of the sky, then I know that I've remembered the fact that the sky is blue. Our minds are used for so many different things. Most people are aware of these uses, but we're only concerned with a few of them when we use our minds. If you're trying to persuade someone, you're trying to convince them that you're right. You're not really concerned with whether they're right or not. You're trying to convince them that you're right and that they should believe you.

If you're solving a problem, you're trying to figure out what you need to do. You're not really concerned with whether your solution is good or bad. You're trying to find a solution. If you're reasoning about something, you're thinking about it in order to understand it better. You're not really concerned with whether what you're thinking about is true or false. You're trying to understand it better.

You can apply the concepts of urgency to a variety of persuasive contexts and audiences. And the results will be just as effective. This may be why many retailers and brands are re-evaluating their entire marketing programs. They're trying to make consumers more conscious of the present and immediate value of a particular product.

The best way to ensure that people buy your product is to understand how people make decisions, and the psychology behind their choices.

There are two basic models of decision-making. The first is known as the ***rational model of decision-making***, which is the approach that most of us take. The second is known as the ***emotional model***, which includes our subconscious reasoning as well. While most people are swayed by emotions, there are three factors that can help you get past your emotional reaction to a product: *price, product features, and product benefits.*

The goal of a persuasive message is to get the person to do something. But the way the brain receives information about a persuasive message, the kind of language used, and the environment in which it's delivered can affect how we receive the message. For example, research shows that a positive emotional response to the message makes people more likely to believe the message. The way the message is phrased, how the message is delivered, and what kind of background the message is delivered in can also influence whether or not we get the desired response.

If you have read any other article about psychology on the web, you probably already have some ideas about how persuasive content works. The way to put your knowledge into practice is by crafting content that uses the techniques to which you are most accustomed. Remember, in addition to being compelling, persuasive content must also be relevant, credible, and trustworthy. Your objective is to create content that is persuasive.

There are four major persuasion tactics used by marketers: *Social Proof, Authority, Scarcity, and Emotional Appeals.* These are the strategies companies like **Amazon, eBay, Walmart, Nike,** and **Zappos** use to persuade you to buy their product today.

Let's start with **Social Proof.** This is a great strategy to use when you're persuading a friend or a group of people. Let's say you want your friend to join you on a hike. You could call your friend, ask him or her if he or she wants to go, or just invite them to come along with you. If you see your friend is hesitant about going on a hike with you, then you could suggest that they bring their friends or ask a few people from their office to come along. Of course, you need to be careful because this might backfire if you tell someone to bring their friends or coworkers along, and they think that they are being told to bring a lot of other people. It's better to make it sound like an invitation and not a command.

The next persuasion technique that companies like **Nike** and **Zappos** use are the **Authority Strategy.** This is used when companies try to persuade consumers to buy their products. Companies like **Nike** use famous athletes to endorse their products.

The third type of persuasion used by companies is **Scarcity**. You'll know that this is being used if a company is trying to sell you a product that you don't have time for or if the product is a limited offer. These are great ways to persuade you to purchase something immediately without you really wanting to buy it.

The final persuasion technique used by companies is **Emotional Appeal**. The purpose of this is to persuade you to buy a product. Companies use this technique to convince you that they have the best product or the best service. It's also used when a company wants you to feel that they care about you.

There are three types of emotional appeals that you'll see used by companies: **Autonomy, Incentive, and Pity.**

Autonomy is the appeal to self-interest. This is when the company persuades you to buy their product by making you feel that you are the one benefiting from the product.

The second type of emotional appeal is the **incentive appeal**. This is when the company persuades you to buy their product by giving you an incentive to do so. This is a great strategy to use when you are persuading your friends to buy something from you. For example, you could offer to buy your friend a coffee if they buy a product from you.

The third type of emotional appeal is **pity appeal**. This is when the company persuades you to buy their product by making you feel sorry for them. This is a great strategy to use when you are persuading your friends to start using your product. For example, you could tell your friend that you are giving up the product because you are not getting encouraged for your effort put into making a great product.

Here are some other emotional appeals:

Compassion: When people feel compassion for a product or a company, they are more likely to purchase the product or buy the company's services. Compassion is a very powerful emotion.

Liking: When people like a product or a company, they are more likely to buy it.

Fear: When people are afraid of something, they are more likely to buy a product or a company's services.

Hope: When people feel hope for a product or a company, they are more likely to buy it.

Hate: When people hate a product or a company's competitor, they are more likely to buy the product.

Lust: When people are attracted to a product or a company, they are more likely to buy it.

Once you know what to say, then it's time to make your sales pitch. There are six key types of persuasive messages that can be used to motivate your visitors to act on your product or service:

- **Gain:** You tell your customers what benefits the product will provide.
- **Reward:** You reward customers who buy your product for the reason you initially told them to.
- **Scarcity:** You create urgency and scarcity in the

product by saying when it's available.

- **Authority:** You claim expertise by using the first person, “I,” in your copy, and give your product or service a brand name.
- **Liking:** You show that your product or service has a positive effect on the customer.
- **Love:** You express how much you care for the customer by showing you truly care.

Chapter 8

The Psychology of Choice

The third key persuasive principle is that of choice. If you ask people what their first instinct is when they're looking at a product or service, they'll usually tell you their choice is the easiest one. In reality, though, they're really choosing from a list of other options, and that's where the persuasive nature of choice comes in. When we're presented with a product or service and asked if we like it, we're subconsciously judging its suitability for us as individuals based on whether we would rather purchase it than the alternative. It's the equivalent of choosing the easiest option. So when you're presented with a new opportunity, be sure to take the time to consider all of your options and the psychology behind each of them.

The psychology of choice plays a major role in your ability to sell products and services. Understanding the psychology of choice is crucial for anyone who wants to maximize their profits.

In this chapter, you will learn more about the psychology of choice and how to use it to your advantage.

What is Psychology of Choice?

The psychology of choice is a set of rules that dictate what you think and feel about choices. The rules are subconscious, so we don't always realize how they affect our decisions. For example, we all know that if we want to make a decision, we should be able to think about it for a long time. We also know that if we have too much to think about, we will most likely forget what we wanted to do in the first place.

However, most people are surprised to find out that the most important factor in making the best decision is not thinking about it for a long time, but thinking about it for just the right amount of time. It's important to note that we are not consciously aware of the rules that govern the way we make decisions. This means that we don't realize how they influence our choices. However, as you'll learn in this chapter, we can use these rules to our advantage.

What You Should Know About Choices

When we make a choice, we often think about it in one of two ways: Either we consciously think about what we're doing or we don't think about it at all. When we consciously think about our choices, we pay attention to the facts and information that are available to us. When we don't think about it, we rely on our intuition or gut feeling. If we want to make a decision, we should always choose consciously. We should do this because if we don't think about what we're doing, we're probably not making a good decision. For example, if you want to buy a car, you need to be aware of all the facts and information that are available to you. If you don't think about what you're doing, you're not going to make the best decision. If you don't think about what you're doing, you're probably relying on your intuition or gut feeling to make a decision. When you don't think about it, you're likely to make poor decisions.

What You don't Know about Choices

When you make a choice, you should always be aware of

the following:

- How much information is available to you.
- The level of importance of the information.
- How much time do you have to make a decision?
- Your mood.
- Your feelings.
- Your emotions.
- Your beliefs.
- Your experiences.

All of these factors can affect the choices that you make.

You are most likely aware of what you already know. If you are thinking about buying a new car, you probably already have a list of features and options in mind. The more information that you have, the better equipped you will be to make a rational choice.

Information is not necessarily facts. Some of the things that we consider "facts" are actually just opinions. For example, the fact that your car has a four-cylinder engine is an opinion. It could also be that it has a six-cylinder engine. If you know nothing about engines, you don't know if it's true or not. Most of the time, you don't need to know everything about something before making a decision. You can usually figure out whether something is important by its relative size and importance.

People like making choices, but not all choices are equal. Research from Dr. Daniel Kahneman, a Nobel Prize winner in Economics, has shown that people tend to make choices based on availability heuristics, not utility or preference (this explains why a Starbucks coffee tastes better than a coffee at a corner store).

In other words, if there are a variety of products to choose from, people will pick the most easily available option. However, if there are only two products to choose from, people will make a different choice. This is where the psychology of choice becomes important.

If you're selling a product, you can use the psychology of choice to your advantage by using what I call the *"double-dipping" approach*. The *double-dipping approach* is a strategy that involves using the psychology of choice to persuade people to buy your product or service. It involves offering your customers two options to choose from. You could offer them two products, two services, or two features. The reason why this works is that we subconsciously think of the most easily available option as the best option.

On this occasion, it's better to be double-dipping than single-dipping.

Here's how to use the double-dipping approach:

1. Give your customers two choices to choose from.
2. Let them choose the most easily available option.
3. Make sure that the second choice is more attractive than the first.
4. Ask them to make their choice again.
5. If they choose the same option, offer them the second option again.
6. Repeat steps 3 through 5 until they choose the second option.

Here's an example:

If you're selling a product, you could offer your customers two choices to choose from:

- Your product
- The competition's product

If your customers choose the most easily available option, they'll choose your product. If they choose the second most easily available option, they'll choose the competition's product.

When you ask them to choose again, they'll choose the second option.

If they choose the same option, you can offer them the second option again.

Repeat steps 3 through 6 until they choose the second option.

You can also use the double-dipping approach when you're selling a service. For example, you could offer your customers two choices to choose from:

- Your service.
- The competition's service.

If your customers choose the most easily available option,

they'll choose your service.

Chapter 9

The Psychology of Advertising

Advertising is a *"persuasion campaign."* Advertisements don't just get people to buy what you're selling. They get people to think differently about you and the product you're selling, to act in a certain way. It's not that people are stupid. It's that people are very good at making decisions for themselves. The best ads are those that make people want to do something that they would never have thought of doing otherwise. But how do you create an ad that makes people do things they've never done before?

In this chapter, I'll share with you what I've learned in my years of creating ads.

When you're creating an ad for your business or product, you must consider the following:

- What does the ad have to say?
- What emotions does the ad evoke?
- How can you make sure that the ad gets to the right audience?

- What does your ad have to say about your brand?
- Is it a good ad for your product or service?

Let's start with the first question.

What does the ad have to say? To put it simply, an Ad has to communicate information to people. And the best way to communicate information is through words and pictures. But there's another way of communicating information that is even more effective than words and pictures: *stories.*

Stories are what people remember most about the world around them. *So how do you create an ad that uses stories to communicate information?* Stories are very important because they help us understand the world around us. We can't possibly learn all the things we need to know to survive in the world without learning from others. And that's why stories are so important. They help us understand the world around us by showing us how other people think and behave. When we watch movies or read books, we don't just watch or read the story; we live the story. That's why we remember the stories we've lived.

Now let's look at the second question.

What emotions does the ad have to evoke? An emotional response is the best way to get people to remember your ad. Think about the ads you remember best. What made them memorable? What emotions did they evoke in you? Did you feel happy, sad, angry, etc.? If you want your ad to be memorable, make sure it evokes emotions in the viewer. The best way to do that is to use storytelling. People remember stories because of their emotions. That's why we love stories. they make us feel.

The third question is also important.

How can you make sure that your ad gets into the right hands? This question is all about your target audience. *Who are you trying to reach with your ad?* How can you be sure that the ad reaches your target audience? To answer these questions, you need to know who your target audience is. And for that, you need to understand who your ideal customer is.

And finally, the fourth question.

What does your ad have to say about your brand? This question is all about your business. What does your ad have to say about your brand and what it stands for? If you want your ad to be successful, you have to make sure it says something about your brand. Otherwise, it won't matter if it's memorable or not. It won't matter if it evokes emotions in people. And it won't matter if it reaches your target audience. Your ad will still fail. So, *how do you make sure your ad says something about your brand?* The best way is to make sure your ad is consistent with your brand as an image you want people to remember. It's a reflection of your company, products, and services. If you don't like your brand, you'll never be able to successfully market your business.

So, how do you create a consistent brand? Here are some tips to help you:

- **Be Consistent:** When you're branding your company, it's important to have the same colors, fonts, and design in all your advertising. It will also help you be consistent across social media platforms.

- **Be Original:** You may think that using the same color scheme as your competitor or using the same font as your client is original, but there's a reason why these things work. Your customers are used to seeing them.

- **Keep Your Brand Simple:** When you have a simple brand, it's easier for people to remember. This means your logo can be as simple as you want it to be.

- **Make Sure That Your Brand Is Unique:** People are attracted to brands that are different and unique. You don't have to do something extreme to be unique. You just need to stand out. The first step in creating a successful brand is to understand what you want your brand to be about. The next step is to decide on a name for your business and create a logo. Next, find a web developer or a graphic designer that will help you create a website and ads that are consistent with your brand.

So, *how can you create an ad that uses stories to communicate information?*

First, you have to think about the people who will be watching your ad. *Who are they?* Are they your ideal customers? If so, what are they like? Think about the kinds of stories they like. What kind of stories do they like to watch? What kind of stories do they like to read? What kind of stories do they like to hear? What kind of stories do they like to experience? Once you know what kind of stories they like, you can make sure your ad is consistent with them. It should tell the same kinds of stories as they like to hear, read, or experience.

Advertising is a lot like storytelling. You can use the same techniques for both. You can use dramatic writing, you can use humor, you can use irony, and you can use other techniques that work on a human level. The idea of using storytelling to communicate information has been around for a long time. It's the way humans learn for a very long time. The main difference now is that we have the technology to make it easier to tell stories. The first step in creating an ad that uses stories to communicate information is to figure out what kind of stories you want to tell. This is where brainstorming comes in.

Brainstorming is a technique for coming up with ideas quickly. The idea is to write down as many different kinds of stories as you can think of. Then, read through your list. Ask yourself if any of these stories would be useful for your ad. If so, how could you use them? If not, why not? The more ideas you come up with, the better. You can also use other techniques to help you come up with ideas. For example, you could use storyboards.

Storyboards are like rough sketches that show the structure of a story. The main purpose of using a storyboard is to help you brainstorm ideas. Once you've came up with ideas, it's time to start creating your ad. You have two options here. One is to use a software program.

The other is to do it by hand. A software program would be easier if you have the right tools. I recommend using PowerPoint or cnava. It's easy to use and it will help you create the kinds of storyboards that will help you come up with ideas. Once you have an idea for a storyboard, it's time to start writing.

There are two things to keep in mind when writing an ad: First, make sure that all the stories in the ad are consistent. If one of them is not, then the whole ad won't be consistent.

Second, make sure that all the stories in the ad are interesting. If one of them isn't, then the whole ad won't be interesting. One of the most important things about your ad is its consistency. You want to make sure that all the stories you tell are consistent. That means that they should have the same length, the same kind of setting, and the same type of characters. For example, you could have a story that takes place on a desert island and another one that takes place on a mountain top. The stories might have different characters, but they would both have the same length, the same setting, and the same type of characters. If you want to use different kinds of stories in your ad, then you need to be sure that the stories are consistent. You also want to make sure that all the stories you tell are interesting. You can't just tell stories. You have to make sure that the stories you tell are interesting. This means that you have to make sure that the stories are relevant to what the audience is looking for. Think about it. The main purpose of an ad is to get people to watch it. They will watch it because they want to know something.

What they want to know is what the ad is going to show them. If the ad doesn't tell them what they want to know, then they won't watch it. You need to make sure that all the stories you tell in your ad are relevant to what the audience wants to know.

If you follow these guidelines, you will make sure that your ad communicates information effectively. You will also make sure that your ad is interesting and consistent. The last thing you need to think about when making an ad is how to get people to watch it. This is where the art of advertising comes in. It is the ability to create an ad that is interesting enough to get viewers to click on it. This is a skill that can be learned by anyone.

Advertising is a very broad term that refers to any kind of communication or media used to promote a particular brand or product. This includes advertising on television, radio, print, internet, billboards, and even in stores. The goal of all of this advertising is to get people to want your brand or product. When you advertise, you have a budget that you are working with. You must make sure that your ad is within your budget. If you do not, you may find yourself out of money before you have even spent it all.

Advertising is more than just the media (TV, radio, newspaper, billboard) you use to get the message out there. As a rule of thumb, advertising is a means to persuade, inform, and motivate consumers. And the better your ads, the more persuasive they are. But advertising doesn't work if you don't have a good ad to start with. Before you can start advertising, you need to be sure that you have a great idea or product to sell. Without it, what you are going to show people won't mean anything to them.

When you think about advertising, you probably think about one of three things: *billboards, radio spots, or television commercials.* While these are certainly ways to reach consumers, there's another form of advertising that is much more powerful in today's world. That type of advertising is *social media*. And just as advertising in other mediums, social media ad campaigns also have a few psychological underpinnings. We'll cover the three that matter most to social media marketers: *emotional connection, immediacy, and repetition.*

It is important to know the psychology of advertising. Advertising is not a science. You need to understand what influences people's decisions and what they like. You need to know about the psychology of advertising. Knowing this can help you to become an expert in the world of advertising. You will then be able to spot fake advertisements and decide whether or not to buy certain products. The more you know about advertising, the more money you will earn. Your income will go up if you know the tricks that advertisers use.

Thus, it is very important that you become an expert in the psychology of advertising.

Summing up the psychological principles of advertising in one word is not much of a difficult task. Advertising is like a magic trick. You can use the same trick over and over, but you can't just make it look like the trick is done over and over. The trick is the *emotional connection.*

Emotional Connection

Emotional connection is the most important aspect of advertising. Advertising that is not emotionally connected will not have much impact. Emotional connection is what causes people to buy products. We're not talking about how well the product will work, or how it will help people's lives. Emotional connection is the part that makes people feel like they have a real relationship with the product. The most common way to make this happen is to create a personal connection with the product.

When you think about a product, you can imagine what it would be like to have that product. You can imagine how it would feel to wear it, use it, or eat it. The more you can imagine what it would be like to have the product, the more emotionally connected you will feel to it. But you don't have to imagine. You can actually experience the product in a very personal way. This is what is meant by emotional connection. When you create a personal connection with a product, you feel like you have a relationship with it. It is like having a friend. The product doesn't even have to be a friend.

Chapter 10

The Psychology of Branding

Branding is a set of behaviors, practices, symbols, and words used to represent your business, service, and/or product. People are familiar with the concept of branding. For example, **Coca-Cola** and **Apple** are brands because the public knows these companies and their products. Even people who do not personally know the brand owners often use the names when speaking of the companies. They may even remember the logos of the companies.

Brand is one of those words that means different things to different people. You can brand yourself, your company, or your products. A company can brand itself by making an advertising campaign that promotes its products. This can be done through television, radio, newspapers, and other forms of media. Some companies also promote themselves through their employees. If you work for a company, you can represent it to the public. You can even go to school to become a brand representative. Some companies build their own brands. These companies make their own logos and advertisements. Some companies will even have their own slogans. **Nike** is a great example of a company that builds its own brand. Nike does not rely on a third-party company to build the brand. It owns the brand. **Nike** creates its own commercials and has its own slogans. The slogan, *"Just do it,"* is a very popular **Nike** slogan.

A brand is an intangible that makes us say things about something we're buying. A brand is nothing more than the sum total of all its associations. So the first step is to figure out what you're trying to communicate with your brand. Then, you need to ask yourself if there's anything your product is associated with that might negatively impact the perception of your company.

Brand Management

Brand management is the process of managing the creation, promotion, and maintenance of a brand. The purpose of brand management is to maximize the value of a brand by ensuring that the brand meets the goals set for it. A brand is an intangible asset that is used to distinguish one product or service from another. Brands are often created by their owners in order to create differentiation between themselves and competitors. A brand can be used to build a business around, or it can simply be a marketing tool to help sell a product or service.

Contents Brands are generally created when a business starts up. This is a good time to create a brand because there are fewer competitors and so it is easier to make a difference. In addition, a brand will be a distinguishing factor between the new business and the old. It is important to make sure that this distinction is maintained, as it can be difficult to recover lost brand recognition.

Branding is the way you get your products or services to be known in the marketplace. A brand means a reputation, a good reputation. Most companies have some sort of name or logo that shows the public that the company is reliable and reputable. Your company will be in trouble if people perceive your company as dishonest or unethical. Your company can also be in danger of losing its customers if it does not behave with ethics.

Why does a Brand Matter?

Your brand is the promise that you are going to deliver what you promise. If you want people to trust you, you have to prove that you can deliver. If you want people to buy from you, you have to make sure that you have the best products or services. If you want people to refer you to their friends, you have to make sure you are the best.

And if you want people to pay you, you have to make sure you are worth the money. *A brand is about making sure that people know who you are and what you stand for. It is a promise of quality. It is a promise of reliability. It is a promise of value. And it is a promise of trustworthiness.*

A brand is about making sure that people know who you are and what you stand for. It is a promise of quality. It is a promise of reliability. It is a promise of value. And it is a promise of trustworthiness.

If you make a good brand, people will notice. People will be impressed by your brand. And people will trust you.

You'll get customers and referrals. And people will pay you to do business with you. When people see your brand, they know that you are going to do what you say you're going to do. They know that you are going to be reliable.

They know that you are going to deliver. And they know that you're going to be worth the money.

A good brand makes people feel like they know you. It makes people feel like they can trust you. And it makes people feel like they want to do business with you. The best brands are built on a solid foundation of integrity. They are built on a foundation of values. They are built on a foundation of honesty. They are built on a foundation of trustworthiness. If you are not building a strong brand, you are going to have a difficult time. You'll have a hard time getting customers. You'll have a hard time getting referrals. You'll have a hard time getting people to trust you. And you'll have a hard time getting people to pay you for what you do. And if you aren't paying attention to your brand, then you are going to have a very difficult time growing your business.

Branding is one of the most important things in business. It is one of the things that separates the successful business from the unsuccessful business. And it is one of the things that separates the top-performing business from the average business. If you want to succeed, you have to get good at branding. You have to get good at making sure that people know who you are and what you stand for. You have to get good at making sure that people know that they can trust you.

How to Create a Good Brand

So how do you create a good brand? There are three ways to create a good brand:

Be different – You need to make sure that you stand out from your competitors. To be different, you have to make sure that you are doing things in a way that is unique to you. You have to make sure that you are not just copying other brands. You need to make sure that you stand out from your competitors. To be different, you have to make sure that you are doing things in a way that is unique to you. You have to make sure that you are not just copying other brands.

Be relevant – You also have to make sure that what you are doing is something that people want and need.

Be trusted – Make sure that you are able to build trust with your customers. This is because if they feel that they can trust you then they will continue to buy your products and services.

Other important factors you must never joke with are;

Be Unique – If you want to be able to create a good brand then you need to make sure that you stand out from the crowd. So what makes you different? You need to think about what makes you unique and then try and come up with some ideas of how you could use this to your advantage. You could for example use the fact that you are different from your competitors.

Be Authentic – This is something that most companies forget about when they are trying to create a good brand. The reason for this is that most companies think that being authentic is bad. However, this is not true. If you can get your customers to trust you then they will buy from you more.

How can You Build a Brand?

First, you need to know what your brand is. What is it that you want people to know about you? What do you want them to think when they hear your name? What do you want them to remember when they think about you?

Next, you need to create your brand. You need to create the expectations that people will have about your business

A product or a service is more effective when it is branded. It will bring attention to the brand, which means that people will remember it, especially if they are impressed by the product or the service. There are many ways that you can create a brand. You can advertise the brand in TV commercials, print advertisements, radio ads, billboards, websites, magazines, catalogs, and brochures. The next thing to do is to get the product or service to the consumers. You can get this done by selling your product in retail stores, through mail-order catalogs, and by giving it away at conventions, trade shows, and fundraisers. You can also sell your product online through internet websites, eBay, and Amazon.

In conclusion, your goal is to build trust and rapport with your audience first. The way to do that is by creating an atmosphere of safety and comfort, so they are comfortable sharing personal information with you. The more personal the conversation is, the more you will be able to relate to them on a personal level and create a bond between you. As a result, your audience will feel less afraid to tell you what's going on in their lives and share their needs and desires with you. This allows you to become a trusted advisor who can offer valuable advice and subsequently great product and services.

Special Bonus

SPECIAL BONUS!

Want These 2 Bonus EBooks For Free?

Get FREE, Unlimited Access To These and All of Our New Books By Joining Our Community

CLICK HERE TO JOIN

Thank You!

Thank you for taking the time to check out my work - I hope you enjoy reading it as much as I enjoyed writing it! Authors wouldn't be anywhere without readers like you, so your support **REALLY** means a lot. I'm a firm believer that books don't need to be expensive or difficult to get hold of - so I want to encourage **EVERYONE** to enjoy the pleasure of books - and not just mine.

I would be grateful if you could **WRITE ME A REVIEW** on the product detail page about how this book has helped you. Your review means a lot to me, as I would love to hear about your successes.

Nothing makes me happier than knowing that my work has aided someone in achieving their goals and progressing in life; which would likewise motivate me to improve and serve you better, and also encourage other readers to get influenced positively by my work.

Your feedback means so much to me, and I will never take it for granted.

I'd love to hear from you if you have any recommendations

of your own, so please do get in touch if you've read anything awesome lately.

If you ever have any questions, you can get in touch at sam@samamoo.com.

I want you to enjoy your reading experience; your satisfaction is my number one priority. You are well appreciated for reading this book.

Thank you, have a wonderful day!

About The Author

Sam Amoo is a writer and publisher focused on business growth, habits, decision making, and continuous improvement. He is the author of Sell Like Titans.

He teaches business owners on how to grow and run business at the same time, without getting stuck between the two worlds of growing and running business. He helps entrepreneurs build their dreams, by combining *concepts, ideas, and insights to make problem-solving easy.*

He has trained over four hundred successful business owners, and mentored over a hundred entrepreneurs excelling in digital and online business. Everything he does is fueled by his love for entrepreneurship, wealth development, diversity, and advancement.

Connect with us here:

Instagram: https://instagram.com/_amoosam

Facebook: https://fb.me/samamoo.official

Twitter: https://twitter.com/samamooofficial

LinkedIn: https://www.linkedin.com/company/samamoo

Email: sam@samamoo.com

Other Books

- How to be More in Tune with The Feelings of Your Customers
- Time Management For Busy People

Made in the USA
Monee, IL
04 November 2026

67379304R00095